D1101791

3

Foreign Language

# Teach English as a Foreign Language

*All you need to know to enjoy
a varied and adventurous career*

**SUE TYSON-WARD**

**How To Books**

*By the same author*

*Living and Working in Portugal*

*Dedication: For Mum, Dad and Ed.*

Published by How To Books Ltd,
3 Newtec Place, Magdalen Road,
Oxford OX4 1RE. United Kingdom.
Tel: (01865) 793806. Fax: (01865) 248780.
email: info@howtobooks.co.uk
www.howtobooks.co.uk

British Library Cataloguing in Publication Data
A catalogue record for this book is available from
the British Library

Edited by Myra Bennett
Cover design by Shireen Nathoo Design
Cover image PhotoDisc

Produced for How To Books by Deer Park Productions
Typeset by PDQ Typesetting, Newcastle-under-Lyme
Printed and bound by The Cromwell Press, Trowbridge,
Wiltshire

NOTE: The material contained in this book is set out in good
faith for general guidance and no liability can be accepted
for loss or expense incurred as a result of relying in particular
circumstances on statements made in the book. Laws and
regulations are complex and liable to change, and readers should
check the current position with the relevant authorities before
making personal arrangements.

# Contents

# Introduction

'More than 300 million people in the world speak English and the rest, it sometimes seems try to...' So Bill Bryson initiates his revelatory and witty account of the English language in *Mother Tongue* (1990). In the decade since he wrote that, the pace of increase in English as the world's dominant language has resulted in some awesome statistics; it is now estimated that there are more than 450 million speakers of English as either a native or first language. Additionally, there exist over 350 million users of it as a second language, or a language of official function, such as in India where there are more than 3,000 newspapers published in English. Add to this almost a billion people using, or learning English as a foreign language, and you can see what a staggeringly sought-after commodity you are dealing with. In China alone there are more students of English than there are people in the USA! No other language has ever reached this level of world status, as English is now the accepted mode of communication in international trade and business, science, air traffic control and pop music. Almost all electronically stored material world-wide is in English, and the most widely used language on the Internet is English. The only other language getting anywhere near to challenging it in global terms is Spanish. David Crystal, in his book *English as a Global Language* (1997) predicts that in just ten years' time there will be more speakers of English as a second language than native speakers, and that 80 per cent of the use of English does not actually involve native speakers, but rather two or more non-natives using English as a lingua franca.

So, what does all this mean to the budding teacher of English? Well, if nothing else, it does give you an incredible world of opportunity, both at home in the UK, and on a world-wide scale. Teachers of English are needed everywhere. Probably no other skill can open up to you work possibilities in both public and private education sectors, in-house company work, private initiatives, plus a whole host of related career branches. And although not all jobs you may experience will offer the same levels of security or finance, for the flexible amongst you, teaching English gives you a passport to travel, to experience other cultures, and to be part of this amazing global phenomenon, which looks set to just keep on rolling.

I hope this book helps you to decide whether teaching English could be for you, and gives you the confidence and practical know-how to leap into an exciting new life, be it at home or abroad. Good luck in your endeavours, and do write to me c/o How To Books with feedback (both positive and negative) on your experiences.

Finally, I would like to thank the following people and institutions for their specific contributions during the research of this book:

Rebecca Chapman, Pedagogical Manager, Business Language Center, Austria; Cynthia Mardon-Taylor, Beltring Language Centre; Studio School, Cambridge; Sarah Williams, Channel English Studies; EFL division at UCLES; Diane Hughes, Lancaster; Lorraine Stephens, The Durham Centre for English Language Training; Louise Magnus, Linguacentre Ltd; Teacher recruitment section, The British Council; and with particular thanks to John Priestley of Impact 92, Lancaster, for his continued support over the years.

*Sue Tyson-Ward, Lancaster, 2000*

# Commonly Used Acronyms

A short note on definitions of commonly used acronyms in teaching English. For the purpose of ease, throughout book I have chosen to use TEFL, or ELT. Further acronyms used in teaching/education are listed on page 169.

| | |
|---|---|
| **ELT** | English Language Teaching – preferred in the UK by many official bodies |
| **TEFL** | Teaching English as a Foreign Language – used by most people, and specifically with reference to speakers who live in countries where English has no official status |
| **TESL** | Teaching English as a Second Language – for speakers who may use the language in day-to-day life, e.g. emigrants, or for people in ex-colonies using it in educational, political systems |
| **TESOL** | Teaching English for Speakers of Other Languages – covers both the above, but is less commonly used |
| **ESP** | English for Specific Purposes – e.g. Business English |
| **EAP** | English for Academic Purposes – advanced level for students wishing to study at a foreign university |
| **E2L** | English as a Second Language |
| **EAL** | English as an Additional Language |

# 1

# So You Want to Teach English?

## APTITUDE AND ATTITUDE

So, you've picked up this book thinking you might use a skill you were either born with (your own language), or have acquired to a high level of fluency through study. Perhaps the lure of financed foreign travel attracts you, or perhaps you are really taken with the idea of introducing people to this language, and guiding and encouraging them in their studies. Not everyone has it in them to be a teacher. Think back to your own teachers at school. Which ones were the most successful in communicating their subject, enthusing you, actually *teaching* you something which you carried forward in life with you? How can you tell before you go any further if *you* will join the ranks of good teachers? How can you predict whether you will enjoy the work? In many cases it will not become apparent until you are faced with a roomful of 15 to 30 foreign faces, eagerly awaiting your 'words of wisdom'.

### Aptitude

Chris Kyriacou in his *Essential Teaching Skills* states: 'The essence of being an effective teacher lies in knowing what to do to foster pupils' learning and being able to do it.' But are we born with that skill, or can it be learned? Your TEFL training will offer you plenty of guidance on becoming an effective classroom operator, but how far do personal characteristics contribute to 'good teachers'? Think back again to those school-teachers you remember in a positive way; did they display any of the following characteristics?

- enthusiasm for the subject
- patience
- sense of humour
- fairness
- interest in each individual
- versatility
- encouragement
- creativity.
- good subject knowledge
- empathy
- discipline
- no bias
- flexibility
- good communication skills
- tenacity

You can probably add to the list yourself. By no means would a potential teacher recognise each and every one of these traits in his/ herself, but a fair mix of them will certainly help; for example, not every teacher needs to be able to tell a joke whilst running round the room whooping with joy about the wonders of the past perfect tense and at the same time checking that Joe's aunt is well again and that Kiko's pet dog is managing with three legs! However, versatility and humour do often save you in a profession where nothing stands still, especially when working abroad.

Could you cope if you turned up at 8.30 a.m. to teach Business English to a group of polite Japanese business people, to be informed that you would in fact be covering a lesson for a group of 25 lively young Spanish students who were expecting to do some drama? Oh, and then you'll be taking a group of new intakes on a walking guided tour of the city. Lunch? Can you manage a three-minute pitta bread (no filling, that's all that is left). Could *you* cope?

### Attitude

Yes, you *could* cope if you approach this type of work in a positive way. Be prepared for absolutely anything, be tolerant of other people's less efficient systems and working conditions. Talk, share, help and understand. But remember, the fact that you may be a native speaker of English confers no God-given right to act in a superior way – even more so as a teacher. You may be able to teach in a supercilious manner, but you will certainly not score too highly in the popularity stakes – and don't forget that student course feedback forms could make or break your next contract. Remember, you have a skill your students would like a share of, but you may also learn something from *them*.

### Essential teaching skills

Although you will learn many practical skills during your training, here are a few areas which can contribute to successful teaching; think what they might mean in practical terms, and how you yourself might approach each one:

- planning and preparation
- lesson presentation
- lesson management
- classroom climate
- discipline
- assessing students' progress

- reflection and evaluation.

Other books on teaching you may like to dip into include:

- *Teaching Today, A Practical Guide*, by Geoffrey Petty (Thornes, 1998).
- *Becoming an Effective Teacher*, Paul Stephens and Tim Crawley (Thornes).
- Effective Teaching Skills series from Hodder & Stoughton (1998), including *Effective Classroom Management* by J. Bryson and *Effective Verbal Communication* by D. Hayes.
- *A Guide to Teaching Languages*, by Terry Atkinson and Elisabeth Lazarus (ALL/MGP Concepts series), available from Association for Language Learning, Tel: (01788) 546443. See page 171 for suggested further reading.

## PROFILES OF LEARNERS

You may have a preference for the age group you teach; in many cases you will have no choice. The following sections aim to provide you, in very general terms, with an overview of learner profiles of different ages.

### Young learners

Whether you are teaching large groups on a summer school, smaller groups at after-school sessions abroad, or even individual tuition, younger pupils offer their own particular learning traits. Children find it difficult to concentrate for very long, so you need to have a varied range of activities to keep them engaged. They often consider the classes an opportunity to play about, particularly if they are away from home. Patience and discipline are essential. On the other hand, they are often very keen to learn and their progress can be measured quite starkly, so you do get an almost immediate pay-back factor of satisfaction.

### Teenagers

Learners in their teens up to young adults fall into two camps. Those on courses away from home who often consider them as holidays with the 'interruption' of lessons and school activities. Others may be more conscientious, needing a good level of English either for entrance to university or to fulfil certain profession-linked ambitions.

Teenagers of any nationality are also going through that difficult period in life of the transfer from youth to adulthood, with all the horrendous trappings that accompany it: surliness, acute shyness and embarrassment (especially when made to speak in front of the opposite sex), arrogance, and bitchiness amongst others. You will need to exercise extreme care, understanding, tolerance, but also discipline to keep groups with you, while encouraging individuals to feel they each have something worthwhile to contribute.

## Adults

Generally speaking, adults on courses are focused, well motivated and keen to get on. Some may be learning the language purely for social or leisure purposes in order to holiday or function in a foreign climate on a day-to-day level. The vast majority, on the other hand, will be concerned to achieve a high level of fluency for business, professional or academic purposes. Consequently they are often initially quite uptight about 'getting their fill' of language practice (oral and written) and may consider childish any attempt at language games or fun activities. You need to help them appreciate that a range of techniques is designed to encourage their participation. If you are teaching in the evening, be aware that many students will already have spent a full day at work, and may therefore find it frustratingly difficult to concentrate for the whole night. Many teachers find teaching adults particularly rewarding as they can establish a good rapport, and even lasting friendships all round the world.

## Nationality traits

Although there can always be a danger in stereotyping national characteristics, it is surprising how much teacher feedback points to a bank of certain factors in cultural approaches to learning (which again may differ somewhat between age groups). Here are just a few observations gleaned from teachers who provided information.

- Hispanics – very lively, keen, loud, often the social-leaders.
- French – Baccalaureate students hard to relax, often demand literature and lots of grammar.
- Orientals – serious, studious, like structured approach with textbook.
- Arab nations – can be very demanding, want to do their own thing.
- Scandinavians/Dutch – generally good speakers, very correct, need to be relaxed.

However, as Lorraine Stephens of the Durham Centre for English Language Training suggests: 'I think it is wrong to generalise over nationality groups. Students in Zimbabwe were very keen and eager to learn, but in Yemen I found the students poorly disciplined and hard to motivate. Some of my current students are Japanese businessmen based in the UK. I find them easy to teach and very co-operative about taking part in communicative activities – not the normal stereotype of Japanese learners.' Be ready for anything, then. A handy range of fun-to-read books on different nationalities are the Xenophobe Guides (Oval Books). At about £3.99, they are slim volumes taking a light-hearted look at stereotypical character-istics of various nations. As well as being a good read, they can also be used very effectively as a teaching-tool.

### Mixed-nationality courses

In some ways it is easier to manage the dynamics of the classroom if you sit students next to someone with a different mother tongue, so there is less temptation to chatter in their own language. However, you may need to pander to a variety of learning and personality traits, and watch out for particular linguistic problems. It pays to know how other languages work, thus affording you an insight into why learners may be experiencing problems with certain points (e.g. in their own language does the verb come at the end of a sentence? Do they use the verb 'to be', *etc.*?).

## ABROAD V. UK – PROS AND CONS

Although many see ELT work as the key to working abroad, it must not be forgotten that there is also a plethora of jobs available in the UK too, with somewhere in the region of 600 + schools in operation. Some locations have a higher number of language schools per square inch than curry houses – Brighton, Eastbourne, Bournemouth, Oxford, Cambridge and London particularly. Even away from the EFL hot-spots, many places have at least a token school, but may even have a university offering summer courses or state schools requiring help for pupils who are speakers of languages other than English. And most towns have a share of foreign visitors working or studying there who may need private tuition. So you don't have to trek to Timbuktu to teach your own language – work may be under your very nose.

So, when trying to decide whether to look around this country, or to dash off in search of adventure in the Ardennes and culture in Colombia, what pros and cons should be weighed up?

### Working in the UK
*Pros*:
- not as far to travel, in case you don't like the place/work
- a 'safe' choice in terms of familiarity
- easier to understand documentation, and not as difficult to stand your ground over pay and conditions – at least in terms of the language of negotiation or recourse to external clarification
- work may be on your own doorstep
- less total upheaval for many people
- large demand for teachers over the summer – an ideal way to get started.

*Cons*:
- not an exotic choice – Cambridge is lovely but it's not exactly Cuba!
- living expenses may be higher, particularly in the main EFL areas (Oxford, Cambridge, London)
- wages may be quite low in comparison with the cost of living
- year-round jobs may be more difficult to find.

### Working abroad
*Pros*:
- adventure, excitement, foreign culture
- new tastes, sounds, sights
- relatively easy means of funding world travel
- the chance to get away from it all (whatever 'it' might be!)
- more clement climates
- friendships around the world
- cheap living in many places.

*Cons:*
- bureaucracy headaches, red tape
- language barriers, especially if any officialdom problems, or disputing contracts
- illness – local health systems may not be as accessible or efficient as you are used to
- pay may be much lower than you expect
- social restrictions in certain parts of the world, particularly for women

- new cultural systems to integrate into
- in some cases, a long way from home
- increasing demands in some areas for advanced qualifications.

In fact, when you look at the whole ELT situation, there is work to be found to suit everyone's circumstances, deepest desires and personal capabilities – whether you want to teach Turks in Tranmere, or lead the locals through the language in Lima!

## RANGE OF OPPORTUNITIES

The range of possibilities in the world of ELT is limitless. We have already looked at the spread of age groups you can teach, and the geographical network which has few boundaries. The next chapter explores in more detail the various places you could work, and Chapter 8 looks at further EFL-related work careers. Useful publications which may offer you more ideas about the whole TEFL scene are:

- *EL Gazette* – available on subscription, in monthly parts, from EL Gazette, Dilke House, 1 Malet Street, Bloomsbury, London WC1E 7JN, which contains news, views and reviews about the world-wide TEFL scene.

- Issues from the IATEFL (International Association for Teachers of EFL), a professional organisation for ELT teachers and trainers. For an annual membership fee you receive six newsletters, various additional publications, plus access to special interest groups, events and networking. Contact IATEFL, 3 Kingsdown Chambers, Whitstable CT5 2FL. Tel: (01227) 276528. Email: iatefl@compuserve.com Web site: *www.iatefl.org*

- *EL Teaching Guide* (from the publishers of *EL Gazette*).

- *Teaching English Abroad*, Susan Griffith (Vacation Work).

If you are a teacher of another subject who may be thinking of branching into TEFL, you may also find useful the How To book, *Teaching Abroad*, which will also give you ideas about teaching your own subject. If you are thinking of combining some TEFL work with a stint of study in another country, *How To Study Abroad* in this same series is a handy guide to life as a student abroad. Other worthwhile publications for people still pondering the possibilities include:

- *Living and Working Abroad*, Monica Rabe (Kuperard).
- *Working Holidays Abroad*, Mark Hempshell (Kuperard).
- The How To series of Living and Working in various countries.
- The Living and Working series by Survival Books.
- The Live and Work series by Vacation Work.
- *Teach Abroad*, available from Central Bureau (leaflet updated regularly).

General information is available from:

- The British Council.
- The Centre for British Teachers.
- The Council for International Exchange.

Details in Contacts list on page 176. And check out the following Web sites for further ideas:

*www.aitech.ac.jp/~iteslj/*     Internet TESL journal
*www.englishtown.com*     chat areas for teachers and students
*www.wgbb.org*     ESOL for adults
*www.teaching_abroad.uk.com*
*www.tesol.edu/*
*www.europa-pages.co.uk*

Further Web sites on page 174.

## THE REWARDS

You will hear endless stories of the ups and downs experienced by the fledgling (and even the seasoned) ELT teacher. Everyone loves to tell of the horrors of dodgy establishments, the loopy red tape, the demanding students (and also the ones who will not talk at all). So why do these same teachers carry on, especially as the overall drop-out rate is particularly high, due mostly to the low financial prospects?

Teaching any subject can be an extremely rewarding experience, but more so in the case of teaching a language, as you see/hear students progressively operate at higher levels of fluency in a tongue that initially was as alien to them as Martian might be to you.

When you are with people who are eager to learn what you have to offer them, and throw themselves diligently into the learning process, you will experience something really quite valuable in terms of personal satisfaction. To be able to facilitate another person's grasp of a subject and see them progress from uttering a few shaky words to holding a coherent conversation is something akin to watching a child in its early grasp of its new world.

In addition to all this deeper satisfaction, the rewards of ELT work include:

- meeting lots of people from a huge variety of backgrounds and cultures
- proving you can cope in sometimes tricky situations
- developing your people and communication skills
- learning to be independent and often self-sufficient
- being creative
- fun and friends.

One final thought before you go much further: in the book *Freedom to Learn*, Carl Rogers (Merrill 1994), reference is made to research that shows that whilst teaching, your heartbeat rises by 12 beats per minute!

## CHECKLIST

1. Have you thought about why you want to teach English, and what personal skills you have to offer?

2. Have you considered which age group you would like/be best suited to teach? Does it matter?

3. Do you know where you would like to teach? Have you researched different locations?

4. What personal and practical aspects of moving away do you need to consider?

5. Are you armed with suitable publications to help you make informed decisions?

6. Is your heart up to it?!!

# 2

## Types of Institutions and Courses

### UK ENGLISH LANGUAGE SCHOOLS

There are hundreds of language schools located across the British Isles, around 200 of them officially accredited by bodies such as the Exam Boards or the British Council, and large numbers of ELT teachers enjoy short- or long-term teaching careers at one or more of them. For many first-timers the school where they do their TEFL training may provide their first post. Other teachers are happy to move around, working fairly short-term contracts for a number of different schools. And some longer-established teachers find a school near to where they live where they can enjoy a full-time position teaching or as teacher-administrators. Often these are people who may have taught abroad for some time and are further on in their careers and settled back in the UK. Occasionally some of these teachers can tend to be somewhat protective of what they consider 'their patch', especially towards younger teachers coming through the ranks, particularly those on short-term contracts, so gravitate towards teachers with your own outlook – there is always a good mix of personalities at language schools. As with any new job it can be difficult initially as a newcomer. Although you may be brimfull of wacky new ideas hot from your training course, remember not everyone welcomes change so readily. You can also learn a lot from people with established careers.

### Type and size of school

Schools can range in size from the individually-run operation, perhaps based in a private house, through medium-sized organisations with purpose-built or modified premises, right up to the international chains of language schools with branches around the globe. Chapter 4 gives you detailed information on actually finding work, which applies to all types of school. You may well find a small school in your own area, with a (small) teaching staff, which you find suits your needs, and is friendly and welcoming. On the other hand, you may consider your ELT career enhanced if you apply to one of the huge organisations such as Inlingua, Berlitz or International House. Certainly you will have great access to positions around the world if you are already working for a chain-group of schools. Publications such as *EL Teaching Guide* and *EFL Directory* (Europa Pages) list schools in the UK, as well as the comprehensive albeit pricey EARLS guide to EFL schools/colleges in the UK. You can also check *Yellow Pages* (libraries usually keep directories for each region).

## Types of courses

The best way to see what types of courses are on offer at individual schools is to ask them for a prospectus/course information brochure. This will give you an idea about age groups taught, specific courses, exam courses, plus details of school facilities (although it's always advisable to have a good look round a potential school if you can). Some schools may specialise in teaching children, or very clearly defined groups of foreign visitors such as Impact 92 in Lancaster, which has a particular market in providing high quality EFL training for Nordic military officials and business people, including representatives from organisations such as Helsinki Energy and Ericsson. In places like this you may stand a better chance of a job if you have worked with these nationalities before (although, in fact, Impact does not specify this as a requirement). Be clear about the kind of teaching you want but if you are not prepared to be flexible, you may have to cast your net much wider.

## FE/HE colleges

A growing number of colleges in tertiary education (Further/Higher Education) are now advertising for EFL/ESOL lecturers and trainers. Usually the job entails EFL teaching to students from overseas studying at the college, to enable them to successfully complete courses in any subject delivered in English. You may also be asked to develop support resources (materials) and offer training to other teachers. Typical qualifications required for these posts may include:

- degree or equivalent
- TEFL Diploma
- CELTA teacher-training status and experience in DELTA teacher-training

- 3–5 years' experience teaching EFL
- experience of ESOL support work.

Salaries may range from $+/-$ £15–27,000 depending on the exact job profile. Adverts for these positions usually appear in the *Times Higher Educational Supplement* (*THES*), the *Guardian* and the *Times Educational Supplement* (*TES*).

The *TES* recently reported on a growing feud between the private ELT sector and public-sector colleges, the former accusing the latter of offering subsidised courses to overseas students and consequently undercutting the private sector. Principals of private schools are seeking clarification from the Office of Fair Trading over the competition law, in an industry worth around £1 billion a year to the UK economy. While the debate looks set to continue, the public sector remains another solid source of EFL courses.

## SUMMER SCHOOLS

Many of the UK language schools run intensive courses, often called summer schools, over the summer period, catering for a wide variety of students. These courses often prove to be a good pathway into ELT with a school as they can be typically short of their own staff who may be away on holiday, or simply busy with the normal classes. The courses usually run from two weeks to a month or six weeks, and can be for children, teenagers or adults. The vast majority of this type of course can be found in or around high-density EFL operating areas – London, Brighton and the south coast, Oxford, Cambridge, Norwich, amongst others – which are the areas most likely to have a large number of visiting students. It is worth applying to schools in spring stating your availability over the summer months. If taken on, you will be expected to be able to work throughout the period of the course, including in many cases, evening or weekend work. Some schools may provide accommodation for the duration of the course (particularly in the case of large, young student schools), but for others you may well have to find rented accommodation over the summer. This is actually not that difficult in places like Oxford and Cambridge whilst the university students are away. However, you do need to consider this practical aspect as well as budgeting for rent (including a deposit) and living expenses. The wages you receive from a summer course will typically not reward you with great riches; once you deduct your everyday expenses from your net pay it is highly unlikely you'll be left holding a fortune. On the other hand, working hard on a summer course more often than not can lead to further work with the same school after the holidays. It is also a valuable opportunity to make contact with other teachers who can give you tips on where to look for work locally. And despite the hard work, it can be fun, especially if you are on the coast or in places as pretty as Cambridge or Norwich.

You can always tell it's summer school time in the large cities when the pavements are suddenly taken over by hoards of loudly chattering youngsters, all sporting identical knapsacks bearing the name of an English school. Groups of sometimes identical-looking children march on the city centres, six abreast, with dozens following on in a trail. You will soon become aware of local feeling towards foreign visitors; in places like Oxford and Cambridge particularly, the dichotomy between extending a welcome hand to foreign students, and the annoyance of being forced off pavements or trying to avoid the mass of cyclists unused even to being on a bicycle let alone riding on foreign soil, is strongly felt (and in the case of bus and taxi drivers, strongly voiced!).

## Children's courses

Children's courses are often run in large premises such as a boarding school closed for the summer, or a purpose-built building belonging to the language school. It is common for the course to be 'residential', i.e. the students also stay at the building, eating, sleeping and socialising there. As a teacher on this type of course you would probably stay there as well, as staff are needed to carefully monitor and supervise meal times and bedtime routines. Typically the students receive formal lessons in the mornings, followed by activities for the rest of the day. These may include sports, drama, crafts and music. There are often opportunities to participate as a sports/activity instructor, which could give you an introduction to this type of course even if you are not qualified to do any of the English teaching. There are also trips arranged, usually by coach to places of interest. These can be a logistical nightmare – keeping tag on 40+ foreign youngsters on a hot day in London is not for the faint-hearted! Often the youngsters consider the course purely a holiday; they are sent by parents who are glad to off-load them for a few weeks, and some of them can certainly be a handful. You may enjoy working with children; working on a residential course may just give you a totally different perspective.

## Courses for young people

These summer courses follow similar lines to those above, except the students more typically stay with host families throughout their time on the course. Classes are usually held in the mornings and afternoons, but there are also trips out, guided tours around the location, and evening activities laid on by the school. It is safe to assume you will sacrifice some of your weekends to accompany students on coach trips, and you may also be relied on to lead evening activities on a rota basis. However, your working day may finish around 3 pm, often with a free afternoon each week. Some of the groups who come across for the summer consist of students who desperately need to improve their English for university entrance (such as French baccalaureate students); for many others it is seen as an opportunity to have a nice holiday away from parents, with the chance to meet young people from other countries. Romance abounds, with tears on departure.

## Courses for adults

Adult learners also appear in the summer, usually on courses of two to four weeks. Often you will find a wide variety of nationalities in one group, and sometimes a variation on levels of competence, however much the school has tried to assess the students on arrival. These courses can be immensely enjoyable, not least because the social side of the course (evenings out, cultural activities) can build up a great rapport and group dynamic. The majority of students are very keen to learn, and you may discover a myriad of ways to help them do so, both inside and outside the classroom, including trips round supermarkets, visits to museums, or attendance at local social events.

## University summer schools

The summer courses on various university campuses work in exactly the same way, with students staying in campus accommodation, attending classes, and enjoying a varied social programme. If the summer weather is good enough, it is not uncommon for lessons to take place outside on the lawns or in the shade of trees. Check with your local university to see if they run this type of course, and how you can apply to teach on it. Positions nationally may appear in the general press.

**OVERSEAS TEACHING**

Take the UK situation described on page 20 and replicate it by the number of non-English speaking countries around the world where people may wish to learn the language, and you should have an idea of the scope for jobs/careers in ELT. Although many countries in Europe now employ a high number of locals in their EFL schools, in China, for example, experts have already predicted that the demand for ELT will become 'insatiable'.

The large groups such as International House have well-organised schools in various countries, with opportunities within the group to move from one post to another. However, the vast majority of language schools abroad are independently run, most of them it must be said, extremely efficient and legitimate. Unfortunately there are also numbers of schools run by charlatan owners who have jumped on the burgeoning bandwagon offered by the world of EFL. In many cases it is impossible to tell before you experience working in a place what it's going to be like, although there are some pointers you can follow:

- word of mouth – talk to everyone you come into contact with, whilst completing your training course, or chatting in staff rooms

- contact the British Council – for lists of posts in their organisation and advice on the local scene in different countries

- guidance from publications – already mentioned so far, plus keep your eyes open for articles on EFL/working abroad in the press. Recent, interesting articles in the *TES* and *Guardian* Jobs Section have included a general look at teaching English, plus an interview with someone who had worked with Voluntary Service Overseas (see below).

For details of finding work and applying for jobs see Chapter 4. Chapters 6 and 7 also deal specifically with practical aspects of moving and settling overseas.

**Voluntary organisations**
Many of the voluntary organisations require people for positions teaching English and training local teachers, or for posts in administration/project organisation in communities with a non-English background. The largest, and probably best known, is Voluntary Service Overseas (VSO).

They regularly recruit volunteers for a number of projects around the world, but in particular in Africa, Latin America and the Far East. Countries currently requiring volunteers include Nepal, Mozambique, Zambia and Vietnam. Although they require teachers to be qualified (PGCE, BEd, QTS – see page 38), you do not need a TEFL qualification itself to teach them English. This means that qualified teachers of other subjects who may be considering diversifying into ELT could put themselves forward.

Placements start at different points throughout the year, and are typically for one to two years. VSO offers pre-departure general and language training, return air tickets, medical cover and National Insurance (NI) contributions. The local employer in your destination country provides basic accommodation and a modest living allowance. In return for the work you invest, you are rewarded not only with a stay in some of the most interesting and beautiful places in the world, but also with the personal satisfaction of working closely with a local community and helping those people to help themselves. However, as one returnee states: 'Volunteering is not for those who cannot adapt to change, or who are addicted to routine.'

For further info contact: The Enquiries Unit, VSO, 317 Putney Bridge Road, London SW15 2PN. Tel: (020) 8780 7500 (24 hrs). Email: enquiry@vso.org.uk Web site: *www.vso.org.uk*

They also offer the service of enabling you to chat with a returned volunteer. Ring: (0845) 603 0027 (local rates) weekdays 6–9 pm. VSO also organises various country-specific open days, and visits many career recruitment fairs around the country.

## Other voluntary groups

- **East European Partnership** (EEP), operating in Central and eastern Europe. Details from: Carlton House, 27a Carlton Drive, London SW15 2BS. Tel: (020) 8780 2841.

- **International Cooperation for Development** (ICD), Unit 3, Canonbury Yard, 190a New North Road, London N1 7BJ. Tel: (020) 7354 0883.

- **The Project Trust**, for school leavers aged 17–19. St John Street, London EC1M 4AA. Tel: (020) 7490 8764.

- **Teaching Abroad**, 46 Beech View, Angmering, Sussex BN16 4DE. Tel: (01903) 859911.

- **Christians Abroad**, 1 Stockwell Green, London SW9 9HP. Tel: (020) 7737 7811. Web site: *www.cabroad.org.uk*

- **GAP Activity Projects** for school leavers. 44 Queens Road, Reading, Berks. RG1 4BB. Tel: (0118) 959 4914. Web site: *www.gap.org.uk*

See also the Contacts list on page 176 for further organisations

## LEA WORK

There is a lot of very rewarding ELT work, available through Local Educational Authorities/City Councils, in UK schools where there is a large proportion of pupils from ethnic minority backgrounds for whom English is not their mother tongue. Although some posts require fully qualified teachers, others are more interested in your experience in teaching English and/or work or interest in ethnic minority communities. Many LEAs/Councils have DfEE funding under a scheme called EMAG (Ethnic Minority Achievement Grant), designed to provide bilingual support for children from those specific backgrounds. Typically these jobs can be found advertised in the *TES* (*Times Educational Supplement*) under the Multicultural/Special Education section; alternatively you can contact councils direct to find out which schools are likely to be looking to fill posts.

### Job titles

Most positions for this specialised English teaching come under titles such as:

- Teacher of EAL (English as an additional language).
- Bilingual support teacher/instructor.
- Primary/Secondary EAL Co-ordinator or Advisory teacher.
- Ethnic Minority Achievement Co-ordinator/Support teacher.

### Skill requirements

Depending on the seniority of some of the posts you may be asked to provide some or all of the following background experience:

- Fully qualified teacher status, invariably a PGCE (Postgraduate Certificate of Education), or BEd (Bachelor of Education), or similar.
- TEFL qualifications.
- Experience of teaching pupils from ethnic minority backgrounds.
- University degree.

- Knowledge of community languages.
- Experience of literacy/achievement-raising projects.

On the other hand, some schools may be just as interested in people with a real commitment to working within ethnic minority achievement services. For experienced teachers, salaries may range from around £14,000 to £25,000 +. Unqualified applicants may be offered in the region of £11–18,000, depending on post and area.

In addition, a number of colleges operating in Further and Adult Education offer ESOL courses to people living locally. It may be possible to get work as a volunteer tutor and gain valuable experience that way. Contact your local colleges, many of them will have an ESOL co-ordinator.

### Where?

Some parts of the country are more densely populated than others with ethnic communities; the following may offer more opportunities than others:

- Hackney Council (London) – where over 75 per cent of pupils in schools are from this type of background. Contact Hackney Ethnic Minority Achievement Service, Recruitment Services, PO Box 10666, London W12 8LG. Tel: Peter Nathan on (020) 8356 7355. Web site: *www.hackney.gov.uk*

- Manchester City Council – a variety of positions/locations working with speakers of languages such as Somali, Brawa, Arabic amongst others. Contact: Ethnic Minority Achievement Service, Palmerston Street, Ancoats, Manchester M12 6PE. Tel: (0161) 274 3425.

- Sheffield City Council – where there are various projects supporting ethnic minority communities. Contact: Education Directorate, Leopold Street, Sheffield S1 1RJ. Tel: (0114) 273 5644.

### PRIVATE TEACHING

Most towns in the UK have foreign visitors living there, and in other countries students are also often keen to have some supplementary individual tuition. Many teachers tutor students privately, either in addition to their normal teaching hours or as part of a general 'freelance' lifestyle. It is certainly an option open to people who have not yet gained a TEFL qualification (and indeed to those who never will!). Few students ever question the credentials of private teachers, although of course having a TEFL certificate may give you an edge if you are in an area where many teachers operate. Private teaching is a relatively easy and smooth system to set oneself up in, if you take into account a number of aspects which could make or break the whole comfort of the situation for either yourself or your student.

### Who does it suit?

As far as teachers are concerned, private teaching gives ideal flexibility, for example, if you have young children at home or if you have other freelance jobs such as writing. It may also be that you have no access in your area to an established language school, or perhaps your general working hours need supplementing (this can often be the case abroad). Students opt for private lessons for a number of reasons:

- extra revision/work towards EFL exams
- confidence boosting – some people are shy of joining groups
- religious reasons – some Arabic cultures do not allow their womenfolk to be in mixed classes for example
- one-to-one intensive conversation practice
- status – particularly for the parents of younger pupils, who like the idea of personal tutors for their offspring.

Personal tuition can be very intense; with one student (or a small group) you can cover a lot of work in each lesson. It can also sometimes seem a lonely working existence, teachers working in relative isolation, with little recourse if things go wrong. However, as Misty Adoniou of TESOL Greece claims in *EL Teaching Matters* (Journal/newsletter available from *EL Gazette*): 'Private tutoring gives the opportunity to put into practice all the terrific ideas the typical classroom doesn't allow.'

### Type of lesson

- **Conversation** – some students may purely wish to sit and talk English with you, without much reference to a textbook. This can be more difficult than you imagine. Although you can choose numerous topics about which to chat during each lesson, you do not want to be in a situation where you're scrabbling around for things to say. Have a bank of stimulus materials you can use as the basis for conversation: newspaper articles, video clips, radio recordings, and keep an eye on what is happening in the home country of your student.

- **Conversation-exchange** – in this kind of lesson the arrangement is that you exchange time speaking English for time practising the language of your student. Often this type of lesson takes place without payment, as the language progress is to the benefit of both parties. If you need to brush up on another language (particularly if you are in another country), this could be the perfect way forward.

- **General language work** – it could be that your student wishes to go over work covered on a course, to ensure full understanding, or wants additional grammar explanations. Usually they will bring their course materials for you to go through with them. Have extra resources to hand to back up the work, to make the learning more interesting.

- **Exam revision** – many students invest in private tuition to help boost their exam chances. You must make sure you know exactly what is required in the exams, and encourage your student in exam techniques. Having a collection of past exam papers is useful – you can purchase them from the Exam Boards. Contact the publications department of the relevant Board. (See Contacts section on page 186 for details.) There are some commercially produced books of sample exam papers now widely available. Check out the EFL section of your nearest large bookshop.

## Whose house?

If you have space and facilities, you may wish to teach in your own home. However, some students may prefer you to go to their home where they will feel more at ease. This may be the particular case with younger students. Wherever you teach, be it in the UK or abroad, you must ensure that you do not find yourself in uncomfortable situations. You may wish other people to be present in an adjoining room, although this can sometimes prove off-putting for student and teacher alike. Remember, when you teach at home you are inviting total strangers into your own house – until you get to know your students take care to ensure your own safety.

If you are going to teach small groups, you may be able to find a nearby venue to rent at a low cost in which you can hold lessons: community centres, church halls, rooms in pubs could all host classes.

**Facilities**

In addition to your main resources, you should be able to provide a large enough table to work on, with sufficient light. You should also try to have a tape player and if you have a video player too you can really exploit a variety of media in your lessons. The room should not be so warm that your student (or you) falls asleep, nor so cold that you cannot concentrate. Make sure you can see a clock, but don't appear to be obviously clock-watching during the lesson. However, when you set a time for the lesson, do keep on top of timing. If your student turns up very late with no valid excuse, you may choose to charge them for the full lesson and finish when you originally agreed. It's best to sort out the rules about this kind of problem before you start.

**Money**

You need to establish how much you wish to charge for your lessons; in the UK this could range from around £8 to £20 an hour, depending mostly on location. Ring up any tuition ads in your local paper to see what people are charging. You should expect to gain less in many countries abroad, where the general cost of living may well be considerably lower. When you take on a student, or group, you also need to be clear from the start how payment is to be made – up front for a set number of lessons/each lesson/each month? What will you do if a student misses a lesson – will you charge them if they do not give you, say, 24 hours' notice? For groups, are you charging per group or per person; if someone misses a lesson do the others have to cover the payment for the whole group? It is important to have all this clear in your head, and even on paper, so nobody is in any doubt.

Remember to keep records of your income from private teaching as it should be declared to the Inland Revenue, although in practice a considerable proportion of this type of financial activity around the world is simply not shared with the tax man!

A useful book on general aspects of setting up as a freelance worker is *Teach Yourself Freelancing*, Hodder & Stoughton (1998). There are also courses on teaching one-to-one, run by ARELS (see Contacts list, page 184). Contact them direct for details of where their training is offered.

## CHECKLIST

1. Have you amassed a list of possible UK and overseas schools to contact?

2. Have you weighed up the pros and cons of a job on a UK summer school?

3. Do you have people you can chat to to get the low-down on overseas work?

4. Could you be happy on a voluntary posting in a less affluent community?

5. Do you have experience of/interest in working alongside ethnic minority pupils in UK schools or colleges?

6. Do you have the facilities/lifestyle to allow you to teach privately?

# 3

## TEFL Qualifications

The qualification requirements for teaching EFL vary from school to institution, ranging from internationally recognised TEFL certificates or diplomas to university degrees, MAs and Qualified Teacher Status. In some places you may get by with no prior formal training, with schools also providing pre-service training in their own methodology. Louise Magnus, of Linguacentre Ltd, in London, who has been recruiting teachers for 20 years, states: 'Get an UCLES/RSA or Trinity Certificate. The other "qualifications" are generally a waste of time and money.' There follows an overview of the types of TEFL training available, to try and help you decide what is best for you.

### CERTIFICATES

The two most widely available and globally recognised qualifications are the CELTA (Certificate of English Language Teaching to Adults) issued by the RSA/University of Cambridge Local Examinations Syndicate (UCLES), and the Trinity Certificate in TESOL (Teaching of English to Speakers of Other Languages), run by Trinity College, London. In addition, there are certificates for those teachers who may wish to specialise in, or have as an extra add-on, teaching younger learners.

### UCLES/RSA certificates
CELTA recently replaced the highly respected CTEFLA (Certificate in Teaching English as a Foreign Language to Adults) which you may still see referred to by schools who do not realise the course has been updated to mirror developments within the TEFL profession.

The course is now a minimum of 114 hours, usually run over an intensive four-week period, or part-time over a year. You must be at least 20 years old to enter the course, and usually applicants are required already to have the standard of education which would allow them entry to Higher Education (A-level/Advanced GNVQ level). You do not need to be a native speaker of English to participate. The course covers a wide spectrum of issues related to teaching and language, and in order to meet course requirements candidates must attend for the whole duration; in addition you must do six hours' teaching practice, observe experienced teachers for eight hours, and submit a portfolio of written assignments. You will be assessed through your continuous professional development, teaching practice and written course work.

The CELTA is offered by EFL schools in approximately 40 countries world-wide. UCLES will issue you with details of the test, plus a list of those schools (exam centres) approved by them who offer the courses. Many other schools also offer training for the CELTA (see *EL Teaching Guide* for comprehensive listing). Prices average around £800 for the four-week course. Further information can be obtained from: The CILTS Unit (Cambridge Integrated Language Teaching Schemes), UCLES, Syndicate Building, 1 Hills Road, Cambridge CB1 2EU. Tel: (01223) 553789. Email: cilts@ucles.org.uk Web site: *www.edunet.com/ciltsrsa/*

## CELTYL – Certificate in English Language Teaching to Young Learners

This is available either as an extension to the CELTA (in which case it is referred to as a Certificate Endorsement), or as a free-standing qualification. If you have already gained a CELTA, the CILTS Unit recommends that you do not enrol immediately on the extension course on completion of the CELTA, but gain some experience first. However, applicants for the Endorsement should have successfully completed the CELTA within 18 months of enrolling on the course.

As a free-standing qualification, the course is designed for candidates with little or no experience of teaching younger learners, particularly in the age groups 5–10/8–13/11–16. There are very many similarities with the CELTA course: 100 contact hours with course tutors, six hours' assessed teaching, eight hours' class observations, and a variety of practical and developmental issues covered.

For all successful candidates on the above courses, UCLES provides details of a free job placement service. This is in addition to any placements you may be offered by the school where you were trained.

Further information from: British Council offices world-wide/ International House schools and other large chain-schools, and those schools on the accredited UCLES list.

## COTE – Certificate for Overseas Teachers of English

This is a specific qualification for practising teachers who already have relevant teaching experience (usually gained in their own country). To complete the course, candidates' own English should be roughly equivalent to the Cambridge First Certificate in English, or Certificate in Communicative Skills in English, Level 2. Courses are generally a minimum of 150 hours, and cover language development, methodology and practical teaching. The CILTS Unit has a list of approved centres around the world who run these courses.

*At the time of writing this Certificate had been put on hold, but may reappear in the future. Check with UCLES for up-to-date information.*

## Trinity Certificate in TESOL

The organisation for these certificates is very much along the same lines as the UCLES set-up. Trinity College has lists of approved course centres world-wide, with basic requirements to be met by candidates; teaching practice, observations, minimum number of 130 contact hours, plus additional lessons in a foreign language. Courses are usually four to six weeks intensive, but some centres also offer part-time tuition over a longer period. There is also the option of pre-course sessions as an introduction to the course proper. Some centres offer a correspondence module in addition to the 130 hours of tutor contact. Courses are available to speakers of English as a first, second, or foreign language. The certificate is fully recognised world-wide. Fees for the Cert.TESOL average around £600–700. Details from: Trinity College, 16 Park Crescent, London W1N 4AP. Tel: (020) 7323 2328. Fax: (020) 7323 5201. Email: info@trinitycollege.co.uk

## Young Learners

Trinity College offers its own Certificate in Teaching English to Young Learners (Cert.TEYL), either as an add-on to the Cert. TESOL, or as a qualification in its own right.

Ask both organisations for all their information on their TEFL courses before you decide which to choose. Then contact a number of schools who offer the training and get details such as length, fees, job placement schemes, before deciding where to invest your money. It is also worth contacting your own local college (state-run), as it may offer TEFL training at a more reasonable rate than the private sector.

## ADVANCED QUALIFICATIONS

For those people who already have an advanced qualification of some sort (MA, PGCE...), or for those thinking of investing in their professional development beyond an initial TEFL Certificate, further opportunities and gains may be made. You may be eligible for more senior positions, increases in pay, a wider choice of establishment or more interesting possibilities both within ELT and beyond (see also Chapter 8 on further career opportunities).

### DELTA – Diploma in English Language Teaching to Adults

The DELTA is the advance course offered by RSA/UCLES under the Cambridge Integrated Language Teaching Schemes. It has been recently developed to replace what were the former established Diplomas – DTEFLA and DOTE. It is also an internationally recognised qualification with a world-wide reputation. It is intended for teachers who already have at least two years full-time EFL teaching (1,200 hours) to adults within the last five years, and who are at least 21 years old. The course is on offer at centres approved by UCLES, who will send you a list of schools and information on the course content. As the training is designed for established teachers, the course covers issues such as language awareness, resources and materials, and evaluation/monitoring/assessment, amongst others, in a deeper and broader way than teachers may have previously considered. To gain the Diploma you must attend either a full- or part-time course of a minimum duration of 140 hours, with assessment through coursework, extended assignment and written exam. Course fees vary from centre to centre, but average around £1,000, whether taken in the UK or overseas; however, shopping around may find you a more attractively priced course.

Although the DELTA requires a large commitment, both financially and time-wise, a lot of people agree that it gives them an edge when seeking more senior positions, or work in EFL-related areas. Nana Challis, a senior EFL teacher writing in *EL Prospects* comments: 'Although it may not suit some people's ambitions, the Delta is becoming more and more of a requirement. It may not open as many doors as you expect, but it does provide you with more scope.'

### Trinity Licenciate Diploma in TESOL

The Trinity courses have slightly less stringent entry requirements than the DELTA training, particularly with respect to previous classroom experience. It is a good option for teachers who may have been teaching for some time without any qualification. As with the DELTA, the course is assessed by written tests in conjunction with observed classroom teaching and an oral interview. Although there are more DELTA courses available world-wide, both qualifications are respected globally as the next step in professional ELT development.

## Masters degrees

An MA (Master of Arts Degree) or an MEd (Master of Education), may be a pre-requisite for work in some establishments overseas (e.g. Japan and some of the Arab states). It can also be an impressive addition to your TEFL curriculum vitae (CV), although the vast majority of teachers manage their careers without becoming qualified to this extent. If you already have an MA in a relevant subject (typically English, Applied Linguistics, ELT) this is an excellent springboard to working in ELT. Some institutions also offer courses leading to specialisation in areas such as ELT management, or include a strong IT (computing) component or, at Newcastle University, for example, an MA in Media Technology for TEFL. If you are considering stepping up to an MA as professional development within ELT, check the course you are interested in includes supervised teaching practice; without it you may well not be as ideally placed for a position as someone who has had practical training. Masters courses are normally completed over one to two years; in addition some universities offer distance-learning courses and summer courses. Universities have their own entry requirements and fee structures, although there may be special exemptions available on application. The *EL Teaching Guide* lists Masters degrees on offer across the UK, as well as courses in the USA, Canada, Australia and New Zealand. For further general information on UK degrees visit the following Web site: *www.britcoun.org/english*

## University postgraduate diplomas

These can be useful alternatives to a full Masters degree, have easier entry requirements and are generally more practical and less theory oriented. They may be of particular interest to teachers who wish to work in state education. Typically of a years duration and open to people with prior teaching experience, a variety of courses are on offer across the country. Some courses permit mid-course transfer to a full Masters degree if students so wish, which then entails working on a thesis.

## Qualified teacher status

If you have followed a postgraduate course leading to QTS, plus you have had classroom experience and a TEFL certificate, many schools will be happy to consider you for positions, including state schools adhering to the British curriculum abroad. There is no longer a specialised PGCE in TESOL, but some institutions offer their PGCE students the opportunity to do a short TEFL course during their training.

## In-service certificate courses

Often referred to as 'Advanced certificates', these are designed for practising teachers who may not have time to do a Masters or full-time university diploma. They last on average around three to six months. They are often offered as a distance-learning package, with specialist areas covered, such as English for Academic Purposes, or Young Learners.

## OTHER COURSES

### University pre-experience courses

A large number of UK universities now offer short (one to six months) certificate courses which act as initial teacher-training courses. Similar pre-experience certificate courses are available in Ireland, Australia, New Zealand, Canada and the USA, and are fairly widely accepted as an alternative to the UCLES/Trinity certificates. Before you enrol on a course check the level/quality of teaching in the English Department, including what Diploma/Masters courses are offered. Talk to current students if you can to find out what goes on. Your certificate course should involve teaching practice – it's important to ask first about this component, and don't take on a distance course unless it has a practical element to it (see also page 41). A typical short certificate course of four weeks costs around £500–900.

### Introductory courses

Many schools, particularly some of the larger chain groups, offer short courses as an introduction to teaching, without bestowing the status of qualified teacher. However, at peak times (the summer in the UK for instance) schools may desperately need more staff, and a quick introduction to ELT is the answer to fill their posts. From your point of view, this is a viable way of easing yourself into the profession and even testing whether you're going to take to it (or it to you) without investing too much time and money to start with. The majority of schools who offer these courses are not likely to be official Training Centres, as the course itself does not lead to a qualification. However, this type of training in a large group of schools usually leads to a placement within their organisation (although you will be persuaded to work towards a teaching certificate at a later date). The main schools offering introductory courses include:

- **Berlitz UK**, 9–13 Grosvenor Street, London W1A 3BZ. Tel: (020) 7915 0909.

- **GEOS** (for teaching in Japan), GEOS Corporation, 55–61 Portland Rd, Hove, Sussex BN3 5DQ.

- **InLingua Teacher Training and Recruitment**, Rodney Lodge, Rodney Rd, Cheltenham GL50 1XY.

Additionally, you can find courses in such diverse locations as: The Brasshouse Centre, Birmingham; East Berkshire College, Grove House International, Kent; International House, Lisbon; Leeds Metropolitan University and Portobello College, Dublin, amongst others.

## School methodology courses

These are really a sub-set of the introductory course, and basically just a means of introducing new employees to the teaching methods preferred by a particular school or group. It is particularly favoured by chain-schools, such as Berlitz, who have their own 'method'.

Often one to two weeks' intensive training covers some general ELT theory, added to which is an induction into how the school operates – classroom methods, use of its resources, lesson content and delivery, *inter alia*. Again, this can be ideal for the absolute novice with no previous qualification, especially as you will go straight into a teaching post at the school. However, you must remember there are many views on ELT, and what you practise at one school may not necessarily be acceptable in another. Be prepared to remain flexible in your approach – take advantage of any training to further your experiences, but do not assume an in-house methodology course at the Teachwell school in Blackpool is going to open doors further afield without something extra to back it up.

### CEELT UCLES exam – Cambridge Examination for English Language Teachers

This is a useful, practical exam, based on the kind of tasks teachers have to perform within the classroom. Although a number of schools have been offering this training, check with UCLES to see if it is still available at the time you are interested, as following a shake-up in the management of the CILTS Unit, some certificates have been 'put on ice' pending further development.

### Funding

Usually TEFL Cert./Diploma students fund their own courses, although reduced-cost courses may be available at some colleges of Further Education. There are also some grants available under a scheme called Career Development Loans, run by the DfEE and Barclays, Co-op bank, Clydesdale and the Royal Bank of Scotland. Make enquiries direct to them. Student loans are generally available for degree courses and PGCE training – enquire via your LEA – Local Education Authority.

## UK TRAINING OR OVERSEAS?

Many people choose to commence their training in the UK simply because access to training centres is much easier. Nevertheless, you could undertake a teacher's course (certificate or diploma) in an overseas school accredited by the qualification-awarding body (usually UCLES/Trinity College). This may well be the case for the intrepid explorers who simply wish to take off abroad and get stuck into life in another country. So, what are the pros and cons of one location or another?

### UK training

*Advantages*:
- nearer to home location
- little, or no physical and cultural upheaval
- possibility to gain job placements afterwards
- large number of schools offering training
- access to information and resources.

*Disadvantages*:
- fees – may be cheaper abroad
- not as easy to go on to find work if training is at a level below Cert./Diploma.

## Overseas courses

*Pros.*

- on the spot overseas, gets you abroad faster
- price – because of cheaper living standards in some countries, the course fees/living abroad may be more attractive.

*Cons.*

- a long way to go to discover whether or not you'll take to the profession
- many unregulated schools – do you know you're getting value for money?
- some schools lacking resources/materials
- teaching practice involving mainly one nationality only.

## Distance learning

Distance learning is a means of following a course of study with little, or no, contact with a tutor/other students. In the UK the pioneer of this type of organised study has been the Open University, which has recently moved into ELT training provision. Currently on offer from them is a new MA in Applied Linguistics, with a newly created online support system. Information from: *www.open.ac.uk/ education/ma/applied-linguistics/* There is also a new TESOL MA course attached to the OU's EdD programme, allowing study through to doctoral level.

Distance learning involves you in controlling your own studies, with guidance. Typically you will be given a course pack of materials to follow, with guidelines for assignments, and deadlines to keep for sending in work. Some courses of this type also include a number of face-to-face meetings with a tutor, where you can discuss your progress. There is also usually a helpline number should you need access to advice as you go along.

This type of learning may suit you if you have a lifestyle which will not currently allow you time to attend a full course. However, if you do not get the experience of classroom practice as part of the course, you may be less attractive as a job candidate than someone who has. On the other hand, you will at least have had some background study, and you may feel you want to try your luck in the world of ELT without a further level of qualification. Many universities now offer distance learning courses in TEFL-related subjects, such as the MA offered by the University of Reading (email: CALS@reading. ac.uk), the MA in Teaching English to Young Learners at the University of York (email: efl@york.ac.uk), or the Advance

Certificate in TEFL at Aston University (email: lsu@aston.ac.uk). Developments are also underway from institutions other than the OU to offer distance learning on the Internet. Check out the following site: *www.icdl.open.ac.uk,* although there is divided opinion about its validity. Chris Graham, Director of Saxoncourt & English Worldwide states: 'The main concern is bound to be the lack of any form of controlled teaching practice.'

### Conferences/workshops

Organisations such as IATEFL, BIELT (British Institute of English Language Teaching) and others, run annual conferences and other training events throughout the year. If you are currently a teacher of other foreign languages, the Association for Language Learning (ALL) also has a good range of Inset (in-service training) days across the country and an annual conference. These are great opportunities for both novices and experienced teachers to attend talks, practical workshops and discussion groups on all aspects of language learning and teaching. In addition, there are usually displays of teaching resources, and exhibition stands of all kinds of related organisations (including many you can contact about potential work).

It's worth investing in membership of organisations like these, as you then gain reduced fees to courses and conferences. For details of membership, contact:

- **IATEFL**, 3 Kingsdown Chambers, Kingsdown Park, Whitstable, Kent CT5 2DJ. Tel: (01227) 276528. Fax: (01227) 274415. Email: IATEFL@compuserve.com Web site: *www.iatefl.org*

- **BIELT**, PO Box 1109, Headington D.O., OX3 8XR. Tel/Fax: (01865) 742086. Email: enquiries@bielt.org

- **ABLS** (Association of British Language Schools), Associate Membership for Teachers, 8–10 Tudor Mews, 1 Hawthorn Rd, Willesden, London NW10 2NE. Tel/Fax: (020) 7377 1737. Email: info@abls.co.uk Web site: *www.abls.co.uk*

- **TESOL Inc.**, 1600 Cameron Street, Suite 3000, Alexandria, Virginia 22314 USA. Email: tesol@tesol.edu Web site: *www.tesol.edu*

- **ALL**, 150 Railway Terrace, Rugby CV21 3HN. Tel: (01788) 546443. Fax: (01788) 544149. Email: langlearn@languagelearn.co.uk Web site: *www.languagelearn.co.uk*

In addition to the structured sessions at conferences, you are in the company of hundreds of people involved in the profession (teachers, trainers, writers, course providers...), which affords you a marvellous opportunity to talk and find out more about the ELT world. Many conference delegates I have spoken to admit they enjoy the coffee breaks as much as the high-quality seminars, as they are able to network and exchange ideas with fellow-teachers.

## GOING IT WITHOUT A QUALIFICATION

Undoubtedly, having a recognised TEFL qualification at one level or another puts you in a far more advantageous position in a market which, although huge in terms of customers, is also brimming with teachers vying for jobs.

Nevertheless, for one reason or another (finance, time, personal circumstances, decided action), you may wish to embark on ELT work without a qualification behind you. Whatever anyone tells you, or whatever you read, it is true to say that there are large numbers of people operating in TEFL without prior official training. And by no means are they all 'cowboys', or poor-quality teachers. On the contrary, some people are born communicators and find they make excellent teachers without ever needing training. Indeed, one could also argue that the possession of a qualification does not necessarily bestow everyone with the gift of good teaching.

However, training courses offer insights into the latest developments in teaching and learning, methodology, access to materials, and important feedback from colleagues and tutors.

If you do decide to manage without a qualification, try to make sure you keep abreast of what is happening in the ELT world by regular reading of textbooks and journals and, if you can, join organisations such as those listed in the previous section, which give you access to newsletters, focus groups and conferences.

Although your market may be narrower than for the majority of teachers, you will definitely find work, be it privately or in smaller schools. If you build up a solid profile of TEFL work, you may even find larger schools valuing your experience and offering you work as cover-supply, or in the peak summer months. If you become more established within a particular school, you may be offered training with them at a reduced rate, which would definitely be worth considering.

## CHECKLIST

1. Do you have all the relevant information you need to help you decide which qualification is best for you?

2. Have you found out where courses are held, and contacted schools for further details?

3. Do you already hold a qualification; do you need additional study to upgrade it?

4. Have you weighed up the pros and cons for yourself of UK/ overseas training?

5. Can you afford to invest in membership of a professional organisation such as IATEFL? If you can, do it!

6. If you decide not to become qualified, what access do you have to materials and information to support your work and own professional development?

# 4

## Finding Work

### APPLYING FOR ADVERTISED VACANCIES

Hundreds of posts world-wide are advertised either in the weekly national press, or through newsletters and publications from specialist ELT organisations. The foreign press (or international versions of UK papers) also carry job adverts if you have access to them. The following papers are known to have a good range of ELT jobs:

- *Times Educational Supplement* (*TES*) available on Fridays. Web site: *www.the-times.co.uk*
- *Guardian* (Education Supplement) Tuesdays. Web site: *www.guardian.co.uk*
- *Guardian International*, and other foreign press.

Additionally, you could send for the following useful publications:

- *EL Prospects* – offers around 250 positions each month, and is available along with *EL Gazette* (see previous details on page 17).
- *Globetrotters*, PO Box 741, Pwllheli, Gwynedd LL53 6WA.
- *International Educator Newspaper*, TIE/E, 102A Popes Lane, London W5 4NS. Tel/Fax: (020) 8840 2587.
- *Overseas Jobs Express*, PO Box 22, Brighton BN1 6HX.
- TESOL newsletter and Placement Bulletin, available on membership of TESOL (see page 42 for details).

### Jobshops

The major ELT associations such as IATEFL/TESOL/JALT (Japan Association of Language Teachers) hold handy 'jobshops' at their annual conferences. There is often an information centre within the conference exhibition, with details of positions on offer around the world. The conference run by TESOL has a specific event called the

Employment Clearinghouse, where you can talk to prospective employers and attend job-search workshops. You will also receive a Recruiting Directory with invaluable job listings. For further information contact Karen Coyne, career services co-ordinator, by email: career@tesol.edu

People are always on hand at these conferences to give advice on applying for jobs. Contact the organisations direct for details about their conferences, and any additional careers information they may offer.

**Web sites**

Increasingly, more schools and organisations are taking advantage of the surge of interest in electronic communication pathways on the Internet. ELT positions are now readily available on sites run by individual schools, or chain-schools and agencies. The problem, as always with trying to find relevant sites on the Web, is that you usually spend a lot of time trawling through totally irrelevant (though possibly interesting) sites, or ones of poor quality, before you find something you really want. Remember that not only are you spending valuable time doing this, but also clocking up a bill for line-time. If you are going searching fairly indiscriminately do it in the evening when time is cheaper.

Not all information on Web sites has undergone thorough checks for validity, application deadlines or standard of school, so be aware that you may have some disappointing attempts at finding work this way; on the other hand you could just strike lucky.

The following sites may kick-start your search:

- TESOL's Online Career Center – *http://career.tesol.edu/*
- IATEFL electronic jobshop – *www.jobs.edunet.com/iatefl/*
- International WHERE + HOW language course finder – *www.language-course-finder.com*
- TLC Search site with on-screen application forms – *www.tlcuk.com*
- The International Educator – *www.tieonline.com*
- BIELT's new site – *www.bielt.org*

Chapter 5 deals with successful applications, but in general follow the instructions for applying carefully, and if you need further information about the post or school before you make up your mind, phone or email the school with your request in plenty of time. When you do send you letter and CV, you may also be asked to enclose other documentation as evidence of qualifications or nationality; never send the original documents unless you really have to. It's worthwhile before you start your quest for work to organise a bank of copies of relevant documents so that you have everything to hand (see page 56 in the next chapter).

## MAKING APPLICATIONS ON SPEC

The other major way of finding work is to do a run of letters 'on spec' to schools, agencies or organisations. What this means is that, although you are not responding to a particular advertised position, you are sending all your details to a number of places in the hope that they may have work to offer you. Be prepared for a certain amount of negative response, but schools who get back to you with 'we'll keep your details on file' may well come up with something in the future. You can always follow those up at a later date with a further letter of enquiry. The important thing is that your availability for work (and your experience/qualifications) is exposed to a large number of potential employers. I used this tactic very successfully myself recently when I needed work over the summer in Cambridge. I wrote to ten schools on spec (from a list of around 30, which I was prepared to work my way through), and the very first one to reply ended up providing me with the work I required.

So, how do you get together your list of possible schools to 'target'? And how do you decide exactly which schools to contact?

### Sources of (schools) information
- Locally you can try the *Yellow Pages* – look under English Language in the classification index, which will direct you to various sections within the main body of the book.

- Your library – usually has telephone directories for all regions of the country, as well as stocking many of the publications mentioned throughout this book. You need to visit the reference section in the library, and be prepared to spend considerable time in there. You will find all kinds of potential sources, in business directories, cultural journals and travel guides. Take plenty of paper and get stuck in!

- Conference programmes/guides and exhibitor information – conferences offer you access to a whole host of potential employers. Visit as many of the exhibition stands as your feet will allow (conferences are notoriously exhausting), and take as many leaflets and hand-outs as you can carry; it's useful to take a small rucksack, as plastic carrier bags easily fill and are a pain to lug around. Wait until you return home to digest what you have picked up, but you will probably find a great deal of what you've acquired has potential.

- Books such as: *EL Teaching Guide*; *Teaching English Abroad* by Susan Griffith; How To Books series of Living and Working abroad guides; *EFL Directory*, published by Europa Pages, regularly updated (4th edition 1998).

- Schools listings – from Associations such as ARELS (Association of Recognised English Language Services), 2 Pontypool Place, London SE1 8QF. Tel: (020) 7242 3136. Fax: (020) 7928 9378. Email: enquiries@arels.org.uk, and BASELT (The British Association of State English Language Teaching), Cheltenham & Gloucester College of HE, Francis Close, Swindon Rd, Cheltenham GL50 4AZ. Tel: (01242) 227099. Fax: (01242) 227055.

### Criteria for creating your 'hit-list'

So, when faced with possibly thousands of places you could write to, how do you make a manageable list?

- Keep to a sensible number to start with – set yourself a target of say 20 to 50 places. Within that range you may decide to write to a certain number each week and monitor responses. On the other hand you may choose to simply mass-swoop on 30 or 40, then sit back and see what happens. Have a contingency plan, or secondary lists in case of disappointing or unsuitable replies.

- Geographical location – where exactly do you want to work, or could you travel to?

- Size of school – small, independent/chain schools offering access to branches world-wide/large networks, including voluntary organisations.

- Type of courses/teaching opportunities available. You cannot tell much from an advert in a directory, so you may want to ring up first and ask the school to send you a brochure, or more details of their operations. Remember though, if you don't have an unlimited budget, phone calls around the country and overseas will soon add up.

- Utilise personal contacts and recommendations.

- Decide whether you want accredited exam-centre schools or not.

Chapter 5 will guide you through actually putting your applications together.

## MAKING VISITS ON SPEC

If you happen either to live or be staying in an area where you know there are language schools, there is the possibility of just dropping in on them to enquire about work. It's not the easiest thing to do – the vast majority of people would probably admit to preferring initial contact on paper – however, there are advantages to the personal call:

- you can look at the establishment and get a feel for the place and the people who work there
- you can also check out the immediate vicinity and ways of getting to and from the location
- they get to see you in flesh and blood, rather than as another name on paper
- you can pick up school prospectuses in person, rather than wait
- you may be able to catch a glimpse of students coming and going – age groups, nationalities, liveliness, *etc.*

If you literally 'walk in off the street', you do need to be prepared in advance, in terms of your approach, appearance and what you take with you. It's no good just turning up and trying to formulate your introduction on the spot, and then not having any personal details to leave. Make sure you are dressed reasonably smartly (see also page 65), and have planned what you wish to say, perhaps something along the lines of: 'Hello, good morning. I'm looking for English teaching work and as I happen to live/be staying locally, I thought I'd enquire about the possibility of work with your school. Is there anybody available who could chat to me about this?'

It is highly likely that the person whom you approach is the school receptionist/secretary, who will not be in a position of influence, so don't go into overdrive at this initial stage; you will be passed on to a relevant person, usually the school manager, or Director of Studies. Often the person in a position to consider employing you will not be free at the time of your approach. You should have with you a copy of your CV and contact details to leave at reception. Make sure you get the name of the relevant people managing the school, along with telephone numbers. Ask when your details will be passed on, and if possible leave your own phone number and convenient times for them to ring you. Take with you copies of any literature about the school, then follow up your visit with a letter or a phone call within a week or two to jog their memory.

Although this method is less effective in terms of time-usage (you should not expect to land a job on the spot in this way), where it is useful is if you are in another country and want to check out a few schools and see what the general atmosphere is like inside.

## PRIVATE AGENCIES AND ORGANISATIONS

An alternative to doing all your own leg-work in procuring employment is to register with a recruitment agency. The way these generally operate is that schools pay a fee to advertise their positions, and the agency tries to match potential teachers to the jobs they have on their files. What you need to do is take in copies of your relevant documents and CV, and have a clear idea (if you can) of where you want to work, and what type of teaching you are interested in, as that will help the agency enormously to search the appropriate files. It is far more difficult if you go in and say you don't mind what you get – the agency is likely to have thousands of positions on its files.

It is unusual for an agency to ask you for a placement fee, as they normally make their money from the payments made by the schools. However, it might be worth asking that right at the start before they begin searching for you. Often you will be subjected to a short interview, which aims to find out more about your experience and preferences for a placement. At the same time you may well be under scrutiny, so make sure you are dressed appropriately and respond in an honest manner (see page 65 on interview techniques).

You can leave your details with as many agencies as you have access to, just keep a note of which ones you have visited, otherwise you may trip yourself up when you receive a phone call from one or another! The following agencies specialise in ELT work:

- **Centre for British Teachers** (CfBT), 1 The Chambers, East Street, Reading RG1 4JD. Tel: (0118) 952 3900. Fax: (0118) 952 3939.

- **English Worldwide**, The Italian Building, Dockhead, London SE1 2BS. Tel: (020) 7252 1402. Fax: (020) 7231 8002.

- **ILC Recruitment**, White Rock, Hastings, East Sussex TN43 1JY. Tel: (01424) 720109. Fax: (01424) 720323.

See also section in Contacts list on page 178.

You could also try any local tutoring agency, who may keep EFL teachers on their books for individual tuition; check in your local *Yellow Pages* for contacts, and see also page 112 on running your own agency.

### Large/voluntary organisations
Major ELT employers such as the British Council, which offers hundreds of teaching and managerial positions on a world-wide scale, advertise jobs in the main national papers, and other ELT publications such as *EL Prospects* and on Web sites. You can apply to these in the usual way. You could also try contacting the organisation on spec. Additionally, you may be able to discuss work possibilities with them at exhibitions, at conferences, or careers fairs. For more details of the British Council activities contact:

- Teacher vacancies, The British Council, 10 Spring Gardens, London SW1A 2BN. Tel: (020) 7389 4931.
  Email: teacher.vacancies@britishcouncil.org
  Web site: *www.britishcouncil.org/work/jobs* and *www.britcoun.org/english/engteach.htm*

For English Language Assistant schemes run by the Central Bureau for International Education and Training, contact:

- The Language Assistants Team, Central Bureau at: 10 Spring Gardens, London SW1A 2BN. Tel: (020) 7389 4596. Fax: (020) 7389 4594; 3 Bruntsfield Crescent, Edinburgh EH10 4HD. Tel: (0131) 447 8024. Fax: (0131) 452 8569; and 1 Chlorine Gardens, Belfast BT9 5DJ. Tel: (028) 9066 4418. Fax: (028) 9066 1275.

Similarly, with voluntary organisations that are constantly on the look-out for suitable volunteers for their many global programmes, keep an eye on the national press, or contact them direct. Look out also for specific journals/magazines or newsletters from organisations; your local church may be a good source of relevant contacts.

## Chain-schools

Some of the larger, and universally recognised chain-school companies include:

- **The Bell Language Schools**, Human Resources Department, Hillscross, Red Cross Lane, Cambridge CB2 2QX. Tel: (01223) 246644. Fax: (01223) 414080. See their Web site: *www.bell-schools.ac.uk*

- **Berlitz**, 9–13 Grosvenor Street, London W1A 3BZ. Tel: (020) 7915 0909. Fax: (020) 7915 0222.

- **ILC International Language Centres**, White Rock, Hastings, East Sussex TN34 1JY. Tel: (01424) 720100. Fax: (01424) 720323.

- **Inlingua Teacher Training and Recruitment**, Rodney Lodge, Rodney Rd, Cheltenham GL50 1JF. Tel: (01242) 253171. Fax: (01242) 253181.

- **International House**, 106 Piccadilly, London W1V 9FL. Tel: (020) 7491 2598. Fax: (020) 7409 0959.

- **The JET programme** (The Japan Exchange and Teaching Programme), The Council on International Educational Exchange, 52 Poland Street, London W1V 4JQ. Tel: (020) 7478 2010.

- **Linguarama**, Oceanic House, 89 High Street, Alton, Hants. GU34 1LG. Tel: (01420) 80899. Fax: (01420) 80856.

- **Saxoncourt (UK) Ltd**, Recruitment, 59 South Molton Street, London W1Y 1HH. Tel: (020) 7491 1911. Fax: (020) 7493 3657. Email: recruit@saxoncourt.com

Following a merger with another large organisation, English Worldwide, facilities at Saxoncourt include a drop-in jobs resource centre, with resident consultants, and access to videos provided by schools abroad. No appointment is necessary and it's worth taking along copies of your CV.

## ADVERTISING PRIVATELY

If you have decided to teach privately, you also need to think up a strategy for finding work. Where will you find your students, and how will they find you? Can you rely on word of mouth, or do you need to think of a more solid advertising campaign? Can you get away with not spending too much money? The ideas below have all worked successfully for various people in different countries.

## Advertising cards

Print out, or write neatly, on to a card an advert which gives out the message without becoming too cluttered. Something akin to the following:

---

ENGLISH LESSONS

(Qualified) teacher of English offers

individual or group tuition

General, business, or exam preparation

Reasonable rates

Contact: Jane Smith, Tel: 01666-333999

---

Fig. 1. Advertising card.

Of course, modify this to match your own circumstances. You may decide to include the price on the advert, especially if you know you can undercut other teachers doing the same.

So, where could you place your cards?

- **University noticeboards** – take enough to cover a range of locations where foreign students may gaze (general boards, English Department, near cafés, in toilets, laundries). Be careful in porters' lodges or anywhere where officials may be on duty; although it is generally OK to put up notices, in some places you may need permission first. Perhaps the best time to do this is during the day when you can mingle with the students. Don't look furtive, but have a good look around whilst you are there, as you will get a good idea of what else is on offer, and what prices are being charged. At the same time a spin-off service you may be able to advertise is proofreading of theses or assignments; many foreign students on English university courses are keen to ensure their work is of a high standard of English.

- **Library noticeboards; community centres** – you will need to ask permission, and in some cases pay a small amount to place your ad.

- **Corner shops** – again there may be a small fee to pay per week, but if the shop is located in an area where there may be a number of foreign visitors living, you could strike lucky.

- **Local FE/adult colleges** – where group classes may already be held. Try noticeboards in the canteen/coffee areas, or put hand-outs in the pigeon-holes of teachers known to work in this area.

- **Telephone boxes** – alongside more colourful ads in some cases (you do *NOT* need to provide a revealing photo of yourself unless you're *REALLY* desperate!).

### Advertising leaflets
Print your own on A5 size paper. You could try a door-to-door campaign, although that is time-consuming and often does not elicit the desired response. Put some around the places listed above, and once you have a few students, use them to spread your leaflets to their friends and other contacts.

### Newspapers and local radio
Place a small ad in your local papers (decide which ones may have the widest circulation) for a small fee. Classified ads are usually charged per line, or per word, so you need to be succinct in your description. Ask whether there are any discounts for a run of ads, perhaps over a four-week period.

If you have a particular angle on what you are offering (perhaps you are a local-raised person with a special story, or are also launching a social EFL circle or similar), you may be able to persuade your local paper to run an article about what you are doing. This will give you fantastic exposure and raise your profile very effectively.

You could try a similar tack with your local radio stations, who are always looking out for local-interest stories.

### Word of mouth
Tell everyone you meet what you are up to, and ask people to spread the word for you. There is nothing more powerful than personal recommendation, so use all channels open to you, including your first students.

**CHECKLIST**

1. Do you have access to a range of publications where you will find work advertised?

2. Have you explored Web site possibilities?

3. Are you fully armed with copies of CVs and documents for personal visits, or mass applications?

4. Have you drawn up a sensible 'hit-list' of potential schools to apply to?

5. Have you located any recruitment agencies and considered how they could help you?

6. Have you planned your campaign for independent advertising?

# 5

## Getting the Work

### SUCCESSFUL APPLICATIONS

Before you launch into your campaign of applying for jobs, try to organise yourself and some space at home in which to do the work. In addition to the letter itself, which we will consider below, I suggest you prepare a stock of the following:

- Your list of schools to contact – organise a checklist with the name of the school, any contact name you have, write the date you sent the letter, and provide a space to note down any monitoring such as a follow-up letter or what response you had (see example below).

| School | Contact | Sent | Follow-up | Response |
|---|---|---|---|---|
| Britling, Moscow | Ana Pavlova | 15/08/00 | 2nd letter 08/10/00 | 22/10/00 put on file |
| Lingo, Brighton | Dir. of Studies | 15/08/00 | | 18/09/00 ring to arrange interview |

Fig. 2. Application-tracking list.

- Your CV.
- Copies of any certificates you have.
- Copies of the page in your passport which shows your nationality.
- Envelopes – A5 or A4, depending on how much you are sending with your letter. You can usually buy cheap office stocks at the discount stationery shops like Stationery Box or Office World.
- Stamps – for the UK take to the Post Office a typical filled envelope that you would be sending and find out the cost. Buy a

stock of that value of stamp. For Europe and the rest of the world, it's usually better to have them weighed individually, especially as you may vary the contents of the envelope. A note of advice when taking lots of letters to the Post Office – sort them first into world region (UK inland/Europe/rest of world) as it speeds up the process and keeps the counter staff sweet.

## The application

It is sometimes tempting to go into overdrive with application letters, putting in every last detail of what you have done and can do. Remember your CV should serve the purpose of listing your qualifications and work experience, and the covering letter should highlight particular expertise you have, or positions of particular pertinence to the next potential employer. It is common knowledge that managers opening applications are turned off when faced with reams of literature. Learn to be concise, whilst mentioning anything that could be of real interest.

Make sure you read the advert properly, if you are responding to a position offered in a publication, and include references to relevant details mentioned in the advert.

If you do not have all the qualifications required but have had some good working experience, mention this in your letter, along with, perhaps, your willingness to take further qualifications if necessary. However, do not labour such points as you may come across as desperate.

## Sample letters

It's worth having a couple of 'standard letters' which you can modify to match each application. If you have a personal computer (PC) (or access to one), it makes life a lot easier as you can copy, edit and churn out letters at speed. But even if you have to write by hand, if you create a couple of master-copies to start with, you can copy them, amending where relevant, without having to start from scratch each time. Some organisations prefer a handwritten covering letter – subscribing to the theory that your writing can speak volumes about your character; try to ensure your script is clear and legible, and keep the letter to just one page. When printing letters from a PC make sure your printing paper is not too light-weight. Around 80gms is a standard weight for general work, white; you can buy a pack of 500 sheets very reasonably at discount shops. That usually works out cheaper in the long-run than buying small packs of 25–30 sheets. The following samples may serve as a prompt for your own 'master-copies'.

### Mary Johnson
#### Language Consultant
20 St Anne's Road, Cambridge CB1 3BB
Tel: (01223) 223578
Email: m.johnson@gemini.net

Director of Studies
Britspeak School of English
10 The Parade
Cambridge
CB2 3JF

17 April 200X

Dear Sir/Madam,

**English Language Teaching**

I am writing to enquire whether you have any positions available for part-time teachers of English over the summer.

As you can see from my enclosed CV, I am a languages graduate and have experience of teaching English in the UK, as well as in Italy and South America. I have taught a wide span of abilities and age groups, and have taught speakers of Latin languages, as well as Japanese and Scandinavian speakers. I have written various language books (mostly French), and am currently working on EFL projects.

I am available to teach throughout June, July and August, and ideally I am looking for part-time work, either all mornings, all afternoons, or a couple of full-time days a week, to a maximum of about 15 hours a week, in order to fit in my writing during the rest of the week.

I have just given up a full-time job in Bristol to return to writing and teaching, both areas which give me great personal satisfaction. I am an enthusiastic teacher, and offer professionalism in everything I do. If you should have any work to offer, please don't hesitate to give me a ring. I can pop in to have a chat with you at any convenient time.

I look forward to hearing from you.
Yours sincerely,

*Mary Johnson*

Mary Johnson ( Miss)

Fig. 3. A letter on spec.

---

## City and Islington College
Ref: 0726 Closing date 28 January

# LECTURER IN ESOL

*(Temporary until end of July 200X)*
**£15,480–26,286 inclusive**

Are you enthusiastic to deliver Section 11 funded ESOL workshops with our Learning Skills centre? Duties may also include some support for groups needing ESOL support on other courses. The post also carries responsibility for developing ESOL support resources. Candidates should have an ELT qualification and experience of ESOL support work.

For further details and job specification contact:.......
Applications should include current CV and handwritten covering letter.

---

Fig. 4. Responding to an advert.

## A CV THAT WORKS

A CV is a record of your education, training, employment and related aspects of your life, such as courses attended, further skills obtained, publications written and, sometimes, personal interests. It is designed to give a potential employer an idea of what you have been doing in life, what qualifications and skills you have obtained, and what personal skills you may be able to bring to a job.

Your CV should be clearly laid out, easy to follow, no more than two sides of A4 and, importantly, honest. The first page is vital as it should offer an instant 'snapshot' of who you are; try to include all the most important details on that page, running on to the next page for previous employment, interests and other miscellaneous details. If you invent qualifications or positions you haven't really held they may well be found out one day, causing embarrassment and possible black-listing. Obviously it is entirely up to you which details you include, so you can choose to omit references to jobs that did not

37 Station Road
Crouch End
London N7 5TT


Mrs G Brown
ESOL Co-ordinator
City and Islington College
New Lane
London
N12 7BR


22 January 200X

Dear Mrs Brown,

<u>Post of Lecturer in ESOL  Ref: 0726</u>

I am writing in response to the above post, advertised in last week's copy of the TES. As you will see from my enclosed CV, I have had previous experience working within the ELT profession, and particularly, most recently, in ESOL support.

I have taught English since 1983, both in the UK, and abroad (mostly in Latin America and in Africa), including two years on service with VSO in Namibia, where I helped to co-ordinate the development of teaching and learning resources within a number of small communities.

For the past four years I have worked as a freelance support teacher with various Local Authorities in the Greater London area, and helped to set up a series of workshops for those involved in the delivery of ESOL support. I therefore feel that I have quite a rounded experience of the type of work your position entails, and am looking now for a permanent post in this area.

I would be more than happy to discuss my experience further at interview. In the meantime, I enclose my CV for your perusal, and look forward to hearing from you in due course.
Yours sincerely,

Brian Bell


Fig. 4. continued.

work out properly, although at interview you may be asked what you were up to during that period (employers often look for the gaps in your chronological history and wonder what you were doing).

Some people like to include a couple of referees (someone who will vouch for your professional or personal character) at the bottom of the CV, others leave them until they are asked to provide them. If you do provide them, do be sure to ask the person first if they mind acting as your referee – there is nothing more annoying for a referee than a letter arriving out of the blue requesting a reference; you don't want to spoil a good relationship, or a good reference.

Once you have created a CV on your computer you can modify versions of it to suit different positions you apply for. If, for example, you apply for a more administrative-type job, or a course-leader position, you may have specific skills and experience you particularly wish to highlight. If you have programmes on your PC which offer quick ways of creating a CV, such as Microsoft Office or Works, it may be worth experimenting with different layouts, although it can be very easy to be drawn into spending an awful lot of time on those experiments. I find it just as easy to set up the CV in simple Word, then look at ways of enhancing the appearance with varying fonts and point size. You could even add touches of colour on headings, if you have a colour printer, as long as the finished product is clearly laid out and not encumbered by too many fancy features: the content must have the pulling power.

If you do not have access to a PC, perhaps you could ask a friend to type up your CV for you and either print out a few copies, or do good-quality photocopies.

### What do employers look for in a CV?
In addition to the all-important background of education and qualifications, employers are interested in the types of jobs you have had, responsibilities held, where you have worked and how often you have moved around. Even non-teaching jobs will be relevant, especially if they have involved people contact/management or administrative work. If you have worked in business, even in the short term, it may prove relevant if you are applying for work teaching Business English. The nature of ELT work means that people are more mobile and teach in various schools during their career, so you should not worry about listing a variety of previous jobs. In this respect it is different to the world of business or general employment where a quick succession of jobs may be viewed with suspicion. It is accepted in ELT that it is quite rare for someone to

# CURRICULUM VITAE

Mary Johnson, M.A. (Oxon.)
Address: 20 St Anne's Road, Cambridge, CB1 3BB.

Tel: (01223) 223578

Date of birth: 23/06/65

**Education**
1977–1984 The Perse School for Girls
A-levels *French, Spanish, English, General Studies*
*Queen's Guide Award*

1984–1988 Wadham College, Oxford
BA (Hons) *French and Spanish*
*College Sports Captain*
*Oxford Blue for Tennis*
*Treasurer Spanish Society*

*1 year in Chile, teaching (plus 10-day intensive EFL course) and travelling*

1989 – 6 months Madrid University
*Distinction in Spanish Language, History, Geography, Culture, Literature*

1989–1990 Hills Road College, Cambridge
Open College Courses: *Psychology, Computing, Business Studies*

1994 International House, Lisbon, Portugal
*CELTA course*

**Other skills**
Full driving licence

St John's Ambulance Public First Aid certificate

Workshops/seminars attended in: *Managing and Developing Effective Teams; Leadership; Conflict Management and Negotiation; Editorial Title Management*

Fig. 5. Sample CV.

**Employment**

| | |
|---|---|
| 1999 – | Impington Village College: *Lecturer, Spanish, EFL* |
| | Mainway School of English: *Part-time EFL teacher* |
| 1999 summer | Studio School, Cambridge: *Senior teacher, EFL summer school* |
| 1998–1999 | Longman: *Editor, EFL coursebooks* |
| 1996–1998 | Trinity College, London: *Subject Officer, EFL examinations* |
| 1995–1997 | HEFCE (Higher Education Funding Council for England) *Assessor for Spanish and French* |
| 1995–1997 | London Exam Board *Assistant examiner/moderator GCSE Spanish* |
| 1991–1994 | Latin America |
| | *Travelling and teaching EFL in various schools* |
| 1990–1991 | International College, Toulouse, France |
| | *Teacher of IGCSE Spanish, French; English* |

**Memberships of professional organisations**

Member, Society of Young Publishers
Member, Canning House (Hispanic and Luso Brazilian Council)
Member, IATEFL

**Publications**

French for Everyone, Browns, 1997
English for French Learners, Browns, 1989

**Interests and hobbies**

Latin music, travelling, exotic cookery, tennis (league team), swimming.

Fig. 5. continued.

### John Edward Smith

Address: 65 The Drive, Burnley, Lancs. BB7 8TS
Telephone: (01245) 688943 (day) / (01245) 875009 (evening)
Date of birth: 16$^{th}$ June 1965

**Education and Qualifications**

University of Hull (1983–1986)
BA (Hons) English and History
(class 2i)

Burnley High School (1976–1983)
9 GCE O-levels
1 CSE grade 1
3 GCE A-levels: English (A)
History (A)
French (B)

**Employment History**

**University of Cambridge Local Examinations Syndicate (UCLES)** (May 1989–Present)

**Examinations Clerk** – a variety of roles including:
- Supervising up to 28 temporary staff receiving and filing marked scripts
- Controlling a programme for the supply of scripts to meetings
- Creating and operating a system for the despatch of materials to centres making late entries
- Supervising staff finding missing marks
- Processing the PET and KET examinations through the complete examination cycle
- Dealing with enquiries from schools into the award of 'No Result'
- Processing examiner scaling and grade boundaries
- Arranging the preparation and despatch of photostat scripts for examiner co-ordination meetings
- Supervising staff checking the transcription of marks from scripts

**Lingualink English Centre, Norwich** (January–March 1989)

**Senior liaison teacher** – short-term cover contract; responsibilities included overseeing induction for trainee teachers, co-ordinating preparation for the pending summer courses; 10 hours' teaching per week

**International House, Madrid** (November 1986–December 1988)

**EFL teacher** having undertaken the CELTA course at the school, I stayed on as a teacher, with particular work in:
- young learners groups
- exam co-ordination
- an active role in summer activity camps
- research into CALL (Computer Assisted Language Learning)

**Interests and Activities**

Cycling, swimming, watching most sports, current affairs, especially transport and planning issues, music.

Fig. 6. Sample CV.

base their whole career in the same establishment. However, if you have had a long succession of short-term jobs, select the most appropriate to elaborate on, and summarise the remaining time.

Even references to interests and hobbies can be of relevance: according to *Fasttrack* magazine for graduates (Spring 1998 issue), 'they can be good indicators of your personality and may highlight strengths that you are not aware of. They can also spark mutual interest with a potential employer. Participation in various sports may show whether someone is a leader or a team player'.

There are different styles of CV you can adopt – those in Figures 5 and 6 may give you an idea. You can also adapt and re-create them to suit your own ends.

## CONFIDENCE AT INTERVIEW

Most people would admit to finding interviews rather nerve-wracking, and even those who claim to feel no nerves at all are probably, secretly, just as nervous as the next person. It is said that a small dose of nerves is good for you, as it makes your adrenaline flow and can sharpen your wits, but how can you ensure the surrounding elements at the interview run smoothly and to your advantage?

### Dress

Whatever your CV looks like (brilliant, or less than glitzy), an awful lot rides on a personal interview, and the first impression you make definitely counts. You should pay attention not only to your main attire, but also any accessories (shoes, hair, jewellery, bags and briefcases, overcoats). Your whole personal 'package' speaks volumes in this kind of situation, and could well make the difference between you getting the job or not. Sloppy appearance smacks of lack of care, organisation and thought; how might this reflect on your professional approach? Whether your interview is directly with a schools personnel, or at a recruitment agency, your attire should give out the message clean, tidy, organised.

- Wear a suit, or something less formal smartened up; for gents perhaps smart trousers with a jacket and tie, for ladies something similar – a dress or clean-cut skirt and blouse with a jacket, or a smart trouser-suit.
- Shoes – sensible, matching your outfit and polished.

- Bags/briefcases – not too big or fussy, after all you shouldn't need to carry too much with you.
- Coat, scarf, gloves – neat and clean, no woolly mitts with raggy holes.
- Hair – neat, clean, tied back if necessary; you want to appear professional, not cat-walk material.
- Accessories – go steady on jewellery, make sure your nails are presentable (your hands will be on show), and try not to wear anything you are likely to be tempted to fiddle with during the interview (such as long, dangly earrings, too many rings, jingling bracelets – all *VERY* distracting).

## Attitude

However desperate you might be for a job, your attitude should ooze confidence without being cocky. Belief in your own capabilities is vital for putting across a positive image, but become too wrapped up in yourself and you may just come across as smug and an individual shiner, rather than a capable person who is also willing to be a team player.

Although your nerves may be playing havoc with your behaviour, try to remain positive. Make sure you arrive early enough, take a deep breath before you go in, smile (without grinning inanely as you walk through the door!) and feel sure of yourself. As Louise Magnus simply states: 'Your personality is more important to your students than all the qualifications in the world.' Lorraine Stephens confirms this: 'We are most concerned to have teachers who fit into our school so the interview is more important than the CV or qualifications.'

Make sure you have prepared yourself beforehand so you are clear about what job is on offer, what you could bring to the position, and why you would like to work there. During the interview try to show an eagerness to join their team without going over the top. Be honest (if possible) when answering any questions, otherwise you may trip yourself up. The difference between getting the job or not may ultimately fall on how much energy you display during the interview. A recent *Guardian* article on interview technique pointed out: 'Interviewers like a candidate with "spar" – one whose interests and enthusiasm are evident to everyone with whom they speak.' The article goes on to mention areas such as varying the intonation of your voice, the importance of smiling, having a positive body posture, and demonstrating how you would approach the position offered. A suggested reader on the subject is

*10 Steps to Energy*, Leslie Kenton, Vermilion Press 1998. Check out also: *Teach Yourself Winning at Job Interviews* 1994, *Teach Yourself Winning in the Job Market* 1998 and *Passing that Interview*, Judith Johnstone (How To Books 1999).

Remember, too, that an interview is an opportunity to find out more about the establishment and the way it operates. It may be that you discover you might not suit the place after all.

## Questions and answers

Rehearse some possible question and answer scenarios before the interview, so you have an idea of how you might respond to particular stock-in-hand questions such as:

- What skills do you think you can bring to the job?
- Tell us about your previous experience with... [younger learners/ summer schools].
- What are your thoughts on... [CALL – computer assisted language learning]?

Have some questions ready to ask them – either memorised or in a small notebook. These could be practical:

- What kind of timetable would be involved?
- What mix of students are at the school – ages/nationalities/ course-types?
- What extra-curricular activities would be involved?

Or more methodology based:

- Do you follow any particular coursebooks?
- Does the school have any specific ELT philosophy?
- What opportunities are there for further training?

Always ask interviewers to repeat or rephrase any question you don't really understand, and if you genuinely cannot think how to answer, say so – its better than bluffing.

## Body language

The main things you should remember are:

- firm handshakes
- maintain eye contact with all the interviewers throughout the meeting

- smile
- focus
- don't slouch – sit up straight
- try not to fidget.


## NEGOTIATING WORKING CONDITIONS

Whether this be at an initial interview, or as a result of a subsequent offer of a job, you should be in a position to seek information, clarify and negotiate the more technical aspects of your work before you sign up to a position.

### Contract of employment

Do not be pressurised into signing a contract until you have had time to scrutinise each clause fully. Ask if you can have time at home to read it through beforehand. This is particularly important in some overseas places. You may choose to get someone to go though it with you (another teacher perhaps, or even a legal adviser). Lorraine Stephens had problems at a school in Turkey, where her contract was in Turkish with an English translation. According to her: 'Foolishly I did not have the Turkish translated. Only (later) did I discover that I was not going to receive the generous package stated in the translation.' Look out for clauses on who pays tax and national insurance payments, what the holiday entitlement is, how much notice you (or the school) must give in order to be released from the contract, whether you are forbidden to work for any other school or privately, and notice of sickness.

If your work is very casual, e.g. a few weeks on a summer school, you may not receive a full contract. Nevertheless, you should ask for confirmation in writing of important points such as working hours and rate of pay.

For longer-term work it is often the case that you will be asked to commence work, with the contract appearing some weeks later. You should also ask for vital information to be put down in a letter to you before you start. You can then consider the full contract in due course.

### Pay

Not everyone feels comfortable asking searching questions about money, but it *IS* important that you know exactly what the financial position of a new post is. Some adverts in newspapers state an annual salary, more so for admin or managerial positions than teaching, and even these can say 'in the region of £x', or '£x–x', so not everything is set in stone.

For short-term teaching jobs it is highly likely you will be offered an hourly or weekly rate. In the UK rates vary from around £8 to £20 an hour (which can actually range from 45 to 60 minutes, so check that out too), depending on the size and location of the school, and profile of their students. Overseas the pay can be much lower, particularly in countries with a recognisably lower cost of living. In addition to knowing exactly how much you will earn, your checklist of questions should also cover:

- When is payment made – at the end of each week or monthly – in arrears, or as you go along? Some schools may not pay until the end of a whole course.
- Do you need to fill in pay-claim forms for hours worked? If so where are the forms kept and to whom are they given?
- Is the school responsible for paying your tax/National Insurance contributions, or are you classed as a freelance/self-employed teacher? (This is often the case in overseas schools, although in the UK, the tax authorities are increasingly reluctant to accept that teachers are truly self-employed.)
- Does the rate of pay include the hours spent on after-school activities or weekend trips, or are these claimed for separately?
- Are there any deductions made from the wages (e.g. canteen contributions)?
- How is the money paid – directly into your bank account (if you have one), or are there facilities for cash payments?
- If you have to travel to other sites/companies, can you claim travel expenses over and above your wages? What about time spent travelling?

It is not always easy to negotiate a better deal financially, especially when there may be another hundred passing teachers who would snap up the work. However, asking pertinent questions about the money side of the job will show that you have your wits about you , and are not prepared to be fobbed off with a second-rate deal. This is important overseas, where some schools can be run by pretty unscrupulous owners.

When it comes to striking a deal over rate of pay don't forget to highlight any past teaching experience you have had, plus make reference to rates you know of in similar schools. Done politely

('...that's a little lower than I was expecting; I was being paid £x in my last position...') you might be able to broker a deal which allows a pay-rise after your first term. In the end it will depend on what you feel you *can* work for, and how desperate you (or they) are!

## Holidays

Also check at interview what the position is *vis-à-vis* holiday entitlement. As a part-timer in many countries you may have little claim to holidays and any holiday will certainly not be paid:

- What entitlement would you have?
- When does it have to be taken?
- What level of holiday pay cover is there?

However, new EU legislation, called the Part-time Work Directive, has recently introduced certain rights for part-time workers, giving them benefits of the same hourly rate of pay as full-timers, plus the same entitlement to annual and parental leave (pro rata). Write to the Department of Trade and Industry for fuller details and, for how it may affect the ELT profession, contact the main ELT organisations.

## DEALING WITH PRIVATE CUSTOMERS

If you are going to teach privately there are still points for you to consider in order to exude an air of professionalism. It's all very well carrying out your successful publicity campaign, but have you thought through the next stages, when people start to ring you up and actually want to commence lessons?

### Telephone conversations

First of all, if your phone number is on all your adverts you need to make sure you are available to answer the phone. This seems simplistic on the face of it, but if you send out an advert, then disappear for a week or are never in the house, more than likely you will miss those vital calls and will have to start again. You could put convenient calling times on the advert if it helps with your existing daily routine. Then make sure you are near the phone, with all the relevant information and your diary, at the specified times.

If it is likely that you have to come and go and could potentially miss calls, think about investing in a cheap answering machine.

Leave a short, cheerful message asking people to leave a contact number and follow up immediately any calls made.

If you have members of the family who are used to taking calls for you, make it clear to them that this work is very important for you, and they should therefore take care to speak clearly on the phone, and not shout for you through the house. This may be particularly important if you have advertised within any companies – what kind of image do you think could be given if there is a cacophony of screaming children, loud TVs and mad dogs in the background? Life is life, of course, and no one is suggesting you gag the children and shoot the dogs, but take this into account and consider how you might deal with it (telephone in a quiet room, out of reach, bribing of children and dogs?).

### Handling the calls

Of course the way you yourself handle the calls will also be vital in securing business. Try to appear friendly, albeit professional; have at your fingertips all the information you may be asked about, which may include:

- price of lessons – hourly rate/ special deals for longer-term courses of lessons (e.g. 12 lessons for the price of 10, if paid in advance)
- how payment is to be made – at each lesson, up front in monthly instalments, by invoice at end of course (for businesses perhaps)
- your policy on missed lessons (covered in Chapter 2)
- what materials your student/s will need.

You should enquire about the students own needs (business/ academic/general requirements), how much learning they have previously done, and how long they are in the area. This should enable you to assess what you can fruitfully do together, and what the long-term prospects are like (which may affect what you charge).

### Arranging to meet

Be clear about where the lessons are to be held – your place or the student's. Perhaps you wish to meet the student in a public place first, as a preliminary introduction. It may be worth suggesting a brief social chat (half an hour) in a local bar or café in order to run through details of timetable, materials and needs. This could take place in advance of making a firm commitment to a lesson, and gives you both an opportunity to get to know each other a little bit first.

Some students may prefer simply to make a solid arrangement for their first lesson, and you'll need to decide where the lessons will take place. Often students will not have facilities where they are staying (unless they are fully resident in their own homes, or with a family) to accommodate a lesson, so make sure you've prepared a space at home.

Once a date and time have been agreed, make sure you (or the student) have clear directions to the house, written down, with your phone number.

### Company work

If you have made contact with a company to do some in-house tuition, again a pre-meeting would be very useful (for all concerned), to sort out the nitty-gritty on length of course, timings, student needs, materials, rate of pay (which should be higher for company training than for individual tuition). Dress appropriately for this type of work – you are dealing with professionals, and they will expect you to be one too.

### CHECKLIST

1. Have you organised your application-making campaign efficiently?

2. Do you have master-copies of standard letters and CVs, ready to amend and send?

3. Have you got (or can you borrow) appropriate clothing for interviews and in-house business meetings?

4. Do you have a checklist of questions to ask about the position and school?

5. Do you know what you should be asking about pay, contracts and holidays?

6. Are you organised for running your own lessons?

# 6

## Preparing for Work Overseas

### SOURCES OF INFORMATION AND ADVICE

So, you've taken the plunge, thrown caution to the wind, and are heading off overseas – destination unknown? Well, perhaps your trip abroad is not quite as vague as this might suggest; but whether you have a job to go to or not, there are various practicalities you must face before you get on the move. This may be the first time you have thought of working abroad, or it could be a repeat visit under new circumstances; either way, the chances are you will need some guidance on the ins and outs of travelling to and working in the particular country you have in mind.

### Work and residency permits

Many schools abroad offer assistance in arranging work permits and cutting through local red tape to get you a legal job. However, this is not always the case, and it pays to have the latest advice on entry procedures to countries directly from their representative Consular Bodies here in the UK.

For those countries now part of the European Union (EU), or included in what is now also referred to as the European Economic Area (EEA), there exists a reciprocal arrangement allowing free movement of people looking for work in any one of the member states.

The following countries adhere to this policy:

UK France Germany Spain Portugal The Netherlands Iceland Finland Republic of Ireland Luxembourg Greece Denmark Austria Italy Norway Sweden Belgium Liechtenstein

However, you still need to adhere to any regulations regarding Residency permits, and you must have a formal work contract on the same basis as for native workers.

73

In other areas of the world the position is not as clear-cut. Often the prevailing philosophy is that jobs will be given to locals, unless it can be proved that there is no one as suitably qualified to take up the position as someone from overseas. As a native speaker of the language it could be said that you are in a strong position to argue your case; having said that, bureaucracy the world over can be pretty tortuous at the best of times. According to Matthew Collins, of immigration specialists Ambler Collins: 'Each application needs to be made on the correct forms and with specific supporting documents. Some governments want original documents, others will accept certified copies. Documents often requested include qualifications, training course certificates, work references, job descriptions, security clearances, and medicals.' See Chapter 9 for a summary of world-wide bureaucracy.

## Possible documents required

- **Passport** – although not required to be stamped in EU countries, still needed as ID (see below for further information).

- **Valid visa** – check with the relevant consulate.

- **Work permit**.

- **Residence visa** – if permanent residence is intended. Can be applied for in the UK from the consulates; expect a delay before issue, sometimes up to six months. On arrival you may also need to have your residency legally recognised at the Foreigners Dept, or similar offices, or at the local police HQ.

- **Car licence and other vehicle documents** – UK/International or EU licence accepted for temporary visits. Green card insurance is required.

- **Medical/insurance documents** – Form E111 is available from the Post Office for reciprocal health arrangements in EU countries.

- **Bank letters** – needed for opening certain types of bank accounts.

- **Student ID** – e.g. ISIC card: useful for obtaining travel discounts and range of reductions.

- **Birth and marriage certificates**.

## Passport offices

Don't forget to check your passport is up to date and will cover you for the period you intend to be away. The regional passport offices are:

- For the North of England and North Wales: 5th floor, India Buildings, Water Street, Liverpool L2 0QZ. Tel: (0151) 237 3010.
- For South Wales, the South and West: Olympia House, Upper Dock Street, Newport, Gwent NP9 1XA. Tel: (01633) 244500/ 244292.
- For the Midlands, East Anglia and Kent: Aragon Court, Northminster Road, Peterborough PE1 1QG. Tel: (01733) 895555.
- For Scotland, London and Middlesex: 3 Northgate, 96 Milton Street, Cowcaddens, Glasgow G4 0BT. Tel: (0141) 332 0271.
- For Northern Ireland: Hampton House, 47–53 High Street, Belfast BT1 2QS. Tel: (028) 9023 2371.

You can also call in person to: Clive House, 70 Petty France, London SW1H 9HD. Tel: (020) 7279 3434.

## Other documents

Copies of CVs, letters of reference (professional and character), professional certificates or diplomas, proof of financial status, and letters of introduction, particularly if from a local person of good standing in the community.

In addition to seeking advice from consulates and embassies (if the country has one in the UK), you can also get general information from:

- The British Council
- The European Commission Office, 8 Storey Gate, London SW1P 3AT. Tel: (020) 7937 1992.
- tourism and trade offices
- the schools offering work.

## Useful publications

The How To guides to Living and Working abroad, TEFL publications such as *EL Gazette*, *Teaching English Abroad* and How To's *Obtaining Visas and Work Permits* by Roger Jones provide useful advice. Many good travel guides also have thorough sections on entry procedures, although you are advised to check your individual situation with an official body.

## Tax and National Insurance

EU countries have reciprocal arrangements which prevent double taxation (i.e. that you end up being charged in the UK and also abroad). Once in an EU country you will need to register with the local tax office/social security system to obtain a fiscal number. This will then allow you to work legally, with contributions being made into the system (which also count back in the UK once you return home).

In non-EU countries you will need to verify your tax position very clearly and make sure your position is above board. Don't rely on the school doing it for you, even if they claim they will – double check it for yourself. Falling foul of work and tax laws can cause havoc and ultimately result in your having to move on. For advice before you set off, contact your nearest Inland Revenue Office, or write to: Inland Revenue, National Insurance Contributions Office, International Services, Longbenton, Newcastle-upon-Tyne NE98 1ZZ. You can also ring the International Services Helpline on: (06451) 54811 (calls charged at local rate). The following leaflets are useful: IR20 – tax liabilities for residents and non-residents and IR138 – living or retiring abroad. Both can be accessed on the Revenues Web site: *www.inlandrevenue.gov*

People *DO* get away with working illegally, dodging laws and flouting the tax rules, usually by teaching privately for cash in hand. You run the risk of harsh penalties, so tread cautiously.

## Social security and health benefits

If you are in receipt of any kind of benefit under the UK system, and are travelling to an EU country, you can continue to receive payments in one form or another whilst you are looking for work or even once in a job, depending on your circumstances. Benefits such as: unemployment payments, widows pensions, state pensions and maternity allowances may all be available to you.

Check with your local Benefits office, or write for advice to:

- Benefits Agency, Pensions and Overseas Benefits Directorate, Department of Social Security, Tyneview Park, Whitely Road, Benton, Newcastle-upon-Tyne NE98 1BA. Tel: (0191) 21 87777.

Useful DSS publications include:

- Leaflet SA29 – Your social security, health care and pension rights in the EU.

- Social security for migrant workers (now a little outdated).
- Leaflet UBL22 – Unemployment benefit for people going abroad.
- Leaflet N138 – Social Security abroad.

Outside the EU these rules do not apply, and you would be advised to check with relevant departments to see what will happen to your benefits whilst you are away.

### Health
If you need to take medication of any sort, make sure you have a good supply before you leave. Ask your GP to note down any generic name for the medicine to help you find it (or something equivalent) abroad. Check whether you need vaccinations for your destination country and get them early enough if you can. GP's surgeries have information leaflets showing the recommended jabs for different areas world-wide. Some schools or countries may require you to have a medical certificate for entry procedures – check well in advance whether this is the case, and ask your doctor for one (for which there will be a charge). Make photocopies of it so you can keep the original safe. It is also worth having a dental and eye check-up before you leave, as often these services are costly abroad.

### Pregnancy
If you are pregnant at the time you move abroad you should ask your own GP's advice about on-going personal healthcare, and check with your local health authority about receiving benefits related to maternity. You may need Form **E112** . This will entitle you to free or reduced-cost treatment for your on-going condition if you are staying in an EU country. To obtain this you must send a copy of your E111, plus a letter from your GP or midwife, stating your expected date of confinement, to the Department of Health, International Branch, Room 512, Richmond House, 79 Whitehall, London SW1A 2NS. Tel: (020) 7210 5318. Try to do this in plenty of time before you expect to leave the UK. You will be informed of your entitlements (within the EU only).

Once abroad, or should you fall pregnant whilst living away, a doctor in your host country will give you all the guidance you would normally receive back home, informing you of your options for treatment (private or state), plus helping you through the physical aspects of your pregnancy. In many countries you will have access to an abundance of fresh, cheap vegetables, fruit and fish products, which will contribute to a healthy pregnancy for you and your baby.

## PRACTICAL MATTERS

Whether you are moving to a foreign country, or within the UK itself, there are many things to consider on a practical level. The biggest logistical problem people are generally faced with is what to do with property they own. Should you keep your property and rent it out whilst you're away, or is your move on such a permanent level that you want to sell it? Do you have family commitments to take into account, or are you in a relatively independent situation?

### Renting out your house

Keeping hold of your property and renting it out in your absence is an option that allows you a base to come home to. But how do you overcome the much highlighted problem of nightmare tenants? Unfortunately, the only way you can guarantee your home will be looked after is to rent it to family or a good friend you can trust; but even here you can never be too sure (and sometimes it is far more difficult to be heavy-handed with people you know well). Even going through a letting agency does not ensure reliable people, despite claims of vetting of prospective tenants. The most professional and seemingly charming people can change totally once they are inside your property. Of course, not every tenant will turn into a problem, and in the end you have to rely on both instinct when you meet them, and luck.

### Letting agencies

An agent undertakes to oversee the whole letting process for you, including: advertising the house, vetting tenants, entering into contract with them, collecting rent, and sorting out any problems when you are away. In return, they usually request a fee in the form of a percentage of the rent (typically around 10 per cent). You may feel this is a lot out of your rental income, but if you have no one who can keep a check on the house, collect rent, or get repairs done for you, it may be your only option.

### Letting yourself

Set your required rental income, based on the going local rate (see your local paper and check letting and housing agents), and what you need to cover your mortgage payments. If advertising yourself, make sure you clearly state the profile of the person you are looking for: professional/sex/smokers or not/pets... When showing people around the house try to get a feel for the kind of person they appear to be. Don't necessarily accept the first potential tenant who comes along, unless you really feel sure they would be suitable. Ask for references from previous landlords, employers and even banks, and follow up with a couple of phone-calls if you are in any doubt. Be clear about how long the let is for. (Contracts should be assured short-hold tenancy types, which only allow an initial let of six months, which can be renewed if required. These give you a safer possibility of evicting bad tenants.) Also clearly state what bills the tenant must pay, and any other relevant house rules. Take a deposit (usually one to three months' rent), which is only refundable at the end of the tenancy, provided there has been no damage, and that all bills have been paid.

Remove anything of value and put in storage if you cannot leave it with family or friends.

## Selling

If you are making a definitive move and want to sell property, seek guidance from local property agents. You can do the advertising and selling yourself, but you will need some legal guidance when it comes to exchanging contracts, but much of the process you could handle yourself if you wanted to. Recently established Web sites allow people to sell homes on the net; check out the How To book on selling your home for further insight.

## What to take

How long you expect to stay, and your purpose overseas, will determine what sort of items you take with you. Household goods, furniture, electrical appliances can all be readily bought abroad. Of course you will always have your own personal effects, but apart from these the following checklist may give you some ideas:

- TVs – if you are taking your own it will probably have to be converted over to the local system. You may also require a completed application for a local TV licence, at the time of applying for your Baggage Certificate. It may prove simpler just to buy one abroad.

- All electrical appliances – you will require an adapter from 3- to 2-pin plug. Once overseas you can buy a stock of 2-pin plugs and change your appliances over. Be careful with these small plugs, as often they easily pull out of sockets.

- Electric fan – if you have one, a must in the hot weather, not only to cool you down, but also a good deterrent against the mosquitoes at night.

- Electric fire – houses in some countries have inadequate heating, if any at all, and the winter can be uncomfortably cold.

- English language publications – reading matter, as books in English can be few and expensive.

- Your favourite provisions – one typical choice is a stock of teabags, as the varieties often available are a weak substitute. I know one lady who asks any visitors from the UK to take her boxes of Yorkshire tea!

- Photos of your family – the locals love to see family pictures and this gives you a conversation starter.

## Clothing

This subject always seems to pose a dilemma, especially when space in baggage is scant and uncertainties about length of stay creep in. Ask yourself the following questions:

- How long am I staying? – short/long term.
- What time of year is it on arrival?
- Will I still be there when the seasons change?
- Do I have any specific health requirements regarding body temperature? Am I affected by heat/cold?
- Does my budget allow for buying clothes once there?
- How much space do I have?

## The summer

The summer months in many countries can be unbearably hot, so if your stay involves being there at this time, do take plenty of cotton clothing (especially white to deflect the sun), cool footwear, and a hat. You will find that journeys will leave you sticky and often soak your clothing, so take plenty of shirts and underwear – washing will dry overnight in this weather. For going out at night a cardigan or jacket over the shoulders is more than adequate (more to keep the insects off you than to provide heat).

### Winter

Although December can still be warm in the southern parts of Europe and other places in the southern hemisphere, elsewhere there is a noticeable drop in temperature. Be prepared for freezing conditions in many parts of the world, including the inland regions of the Mediterranean.

### Pets

If you decide that you cannot bear to leave behind your own trusted companion, then you can take animals with you, but you must make sure they have all necessary inoculations before you go, including vaccination against rabies; check with your local vet. You will also have to take with you proof of vaccinations and any other recent treatment. Advice on entry restrictions to certain countries can be sought initially from your own vet, who will also give you information about the new UK pet passport scheme introduced in 2000.

For further information contact the Ministry of Agriculture, Fisheries and Food, see page 176 for the address.

### Removals and customs

If you have decided on a definite move your next thoughts should include what amount of your own household goods you wish to take with you. Of course, if you only intend to move on a semi-permanent basis, perhaps retaining property in the UK to which you will return at a later date, then you may only require your 'favourite' pieces of furniture removing. A complete house removal can cost on average £5,000. Further details can be obtained from any of the removal firms listed at the end of this book.

### Before you leave

You will probably need to acquire:

- a **Baggage Certificate**
- an **Inventory**
- an **Affidavit**.

To obtain a Baggage Certificate, you need to produce copies of your overseas property deeds (notarised) or a resident's permit, both within 90 days of issue. The Baggage Certificate will allow you duty-free importation of your goods. You will also need a duplicated inventory (translated), which should include details of main items/

smaller, loose items/electricals (include make and serial number). This is particularly important and will save you considerable time at Customs abroad, where intensive investigation and registration of electricals can delay you. The Affidavit, also translated and in duplicate, and again notarised, should state that you have no other property overseas and that the goods listed have been yours for over a year. In the case of recently acquired electricals, keep receipts/ guarantees with you.

Send all these documents to the relevant consulate, from where your Baggage Certificate will be issued. Again, you will have up to 90 days in which to use it. If you have any doubts at all, contact the consulate well in advance of your move for their latest advice; details will vary from country to country.

### On arrival

You may need to sign a declaration stating that you don't already have a furnished residence and that only the items on the inventory have been imported. There may be a charge imposed on your goods by Customs to release them, based on weight and value.

### Travel

Having made the decision to get up and go, your next move will be to consider how to get yourself and (possibly) your belongings over the waters, and this obviously depends very much on your intentions.

- How long will your stay be?
  - is this your definitive trip there?
  - is it an exploratory trip?

- How much will you need with you initially?
  - clothes and personal items
  - furniture.

- Will you need a car with you?

- Are you working to a budget?

- Your exact destination
  - north/south
  - coast/inland.

- Are you travelling alone/with family?

## Air

This is by far the quickest, most efficient way to travel, especially if you have little baggage. Flights are available either through your local travel agencies, or for cheap flights to many world-wide destinations contact the airlines direct, or check out some of the latest cheap deals on the Internet.

- *www.travelocity.co.uk*
- *www.travelselect.com*
- *www.travelstore.com*
- *www.uTravel.co.uk*
- *www.easyjet.com*
- *www.go-fly.com*
- *www.ryanair.com*

Equally so, on offer over the winter are cheap long-stay holidays, designed for those people wishing to escape the British winter blues, but certainly affording an ideal opportunity to reach destinations in sunnier climes: they provide cheap, good accommodation in large hotel complexes whilst you look around for alternatives. I chose this option on one visit to the Algarve, and ended up paying the equivalent of about £25 a week for the lovely apartment I was in (including gas, water and electricity), over the winter until I moved on.

## Ferry

If you are taking your car, you have a number of alternative ferry routes:

- To a French port such as St Malo, Calais or Caen, amongst others, and drive on to your destination country.

- To Santander or Bilbao, N. Spain: 24-hour crossing and drive on to locations in Iberia and down to North Africa.

Contact Brittany Ferries (Santander or via France). Tel: (0990) 360360 or P&O Ferries (for Bilbao). Tel: (0990) 980980. The latest leaflet will be available from travel agents.

Costs vary according to season, number of passengers travelling in vehicle and size of vehicle.

## Trains and coaches

A great journey for the more adventurous is by train. Take Eurostar from London to Paris and then trains to other European destinations. Alternatively, catch a National Express coach from London Victoria.

Details from:

- Eurostar – Waterloo Station, London, and all main BR stations. Tel: (01233) 617575.

- Le Shuttle Tel: (0990) 353535.

- BR Continental Section, Victoria Station, London SW1. Tel: (020) 7834 2345.

- National Express Coaches (Eurolines), Victoria Coach Station, Buckingham Palace Rd, London SW1. Tel: (020) 7730 0202.

## FAMILY CONSIDERATIONS

For some people the decision to move abroad to work can be all-pervading, and sometimes the overriding excitement and anticipation needs to be tempered with consideration of how the move may affect other family members.

### Parents

Whether or not you live at home with your parents, you may need to assure them that you will take a sensible approach to your travels, and that you have a relatively secure destination to travel to. All parents worry, some more than others, and the concern may be particularly acute if you are female. Sharing details of your intended work/locations with them may help to alleviate some of the uncertainties about where you are off to. You may be able to arrange for them, or other family members, to visit you at some point, so they can see for themselves where you are. Whilst you are abroad make regular contact with your family, to keep them positive about what you are doing.

### Spouse and children

If your decision to move away involves uprooting your whole family, there are far more considerations to take into account:

- What will your spouse do for a living?
- Schooling for children?
- Fitting into a new lifestyle/culture?
- Taking your family away from friends and familiarity.
- Finding suitable accommodation (see also next chapter).
- Coping if things go wrong.

Many families each year make the move to warmer climes, particularly to Mediterranean destinations; the allure of a more clement climate and gentler way of life is extremely strong. However, problems do arise when one partner finds him/herself without work, which could be a reversal of the former situation. Frustration, anger, depression can all intrude on family life, and great numbers of ex-patriot hopefuls too quickly succumb to the cheap booze available at all hours in many countries. All too soon life can spiral downwards, affecting the whole family in a disastrous way. Families break up at alarming rates in typical ex-pat hotspots. What can you do to avoid these problems from the start?

- Discuss with the whole family before you leave what changes are likely to occur and how you will all deal with them.

- Explore the possibilities of work for your spouse – what skills can be built on?

- Ensure you do things together as a family, so that no one feels neglected. This can be particularly rewarding if you take up an activity involving you in the local community (church, language classes, sport, travel).

Try to take enough money with you to tide you over the first few months until work is providing you with a living. You may have to live frugally for a while, but allow small treats for the family to keep up morale. Although a move abroad can be exciting for everyone, it can also be bewildering and hard work. Plan in advance to soften the low points.

For more thoughts on these issues, try the Culture Shock! Guides from Kuperard press, particularly *A Parent's Guide* and *A Wife's Guide*, plus from the same publisher: *Living and Working Abroad* by Monica Rabe.

### Grown-up children

You may be at a point in life where your children have already left home, and you have decided to fly the nest yourself. Children can react in two very distinct ways: either they will be extremely supportive and think what you are doing is great (even quite 'cool'), or they'll respond with incredulity and wonder what on earth you're up to! This can be a signal of various emotions:

- Their secure life is suddenly being shaken – parents don't move away from their children.

- Parents do not behave like students, trekking off to foreign soil, unless they're hippies, do they?

- What is going to happen to the family home/parents' digs – no place to drop in on anymore (nowhere to bring home dirty washing!).

- How will they contact you when they have problems or need some cash?

You may need to reassure them about your plans – but after all if this is something you really want to do, who should stand in your way? Try to turn their concerns into positives – possibilities of visits abroad, parent with street-cred, contact maintained via Internet (you can get yourself a Hotmail address, which you can access on any computer around the world), introduce them to the wonders of the local launderette!

## LEARNING THE LANGUAGE

You really should try to learn some of the language of your destination country in advance, even the simple basics – everyday greetings and pleasantries. Although some languages are very difficult, you *can* pick up a smattering with a bit of effort. The best way to do this is to enrol on a short language course at your local college. Some colleges run holiday language courses, usually for six to ten weeks, and these will give you enough to start communicating. I used to run combined language and culture courses, which proved very popular, and you may find something similar in your own region.

Not every area offers every language as a course. If you have problems finding a course in your area, drop me a line c/o The Association for Language Learning, 150 Railway Terrace, Rugby CV21 3HN, and I'll see how I can help. If you can't get onto a course the next best thing is to follow a coursebook with a tape. There are many learner-friendly courses around these days.

When you do go abroad find a place in your packing for your book, tape and a phrase book and dictionary – continue your endeavours once out there. You can also try out conversation exchange once you are settled in your new country – you give a session of English in exchange for a session in the local language. This can prove very satisfactory, and increases your social circle too. The school where you are teaching may have local teachers or students willing to do this.

### Recommended language coursebooks

- Teach Yourself range: contact Fiona Davenport, Teach Yourself Languages, Hodder & Stoughton Educational, 338 Euston Road, London NW1 3BH. Tel: (020) 7873 6000.

- Routledge Colloquials series: catalogues available in most large bookshops. Both the above series offer around 60 languages, covering the more common French, Spanish, German, through to the likes of Serbo-Croat, Chinese and Tagalog.

- BBC books – a good selection of the main languages, with tapes and videos, and linked to radio and TV programmes.

- Hugos publications, particularly the '...in 3 months' series.

There are many other books on sale now – try to get a set which has accompanying tapes. For handiness, small phrase books will also be of use, and will fit neatly into a bag or pocket.

### PREPARING PROFESSIONALLY

Before you make your move abroad (or indeed a move to a different part of the UK), there are certain preparations you can make in anticipation of your new job.

### Training

If you haven't already done any formal TEFL training prior to applying for a job, you may wish to consider it as an option now. Alternatively, you may be offered a position subject to your undertaking certain initial (or further) qualifications. If this is the case, make sure you do it, as your job may no longer be on offer if you have not fulfilled this part of the agreement.

If you have been offered a training position, or a post in management/EFL administration, look around for courses you could do to further add to your existing knowledge and skills. Even general courses at your local college/nightschool will provide an additional boost to your professional make-up (computing, accounts, marketing, communication skills, *etc.*).

### Background reading
You can help yourself immensely by doing some reading in the time leading up to your departure:

- general books about the country/place in which you'll be living
- guide books to life and culture overseas, or different parts of the UK
- language books
- your TEFL training books
- information from the school (if applicable)
- information from the consulates or tourism offices
- Check out also the Web site of the National Geographic magazine *www.nationalgeographic.com* which, in addition to giving you information on countries, can also provide you with interesting articles for use in your teaching.

### Materials
If you are going off to a school, it is worth checking whether they follow any particular coursebooks, which you then should get hold of and study if you can, so that you have an idea of what you could be teaching. Many schools use a variety of books, which may prove difficult to get hold of (or expensive), but most EFL textbooks follow a fairly consistent pattern of form and content. If you know you will be teaching to an exam, such as the Cambridge First Certificate, get hold of past exam papers and make sure you have an idea of what is expected of the students.

Although you may not have enough space to carry many materials or books with you, what you can usefully pack is a file of pre-prepared games, activities, ice-breakers and even ideas for lesson plans. Anything you can do now that will save you some time later on will definitely assist you when you finally get in the thick of it.

### Documentation
Get a file together with copies of all your relevant certificates of qualification, copies of your CV, any letters of reference, copies of

birth certificate, passport, driving licence. You may find you will want to move to other jobs once you are on the move, so if you have your 'mobile office' with you, with sufficient copies of documents, you won't have to scrabble around searching for relevant pieces of paper. Be efficient and think ahead.

## CHECKLIST

1. Have you contacted official bodies for advice on entry requirements and information on the country you will be visiting?

2. What is your tax/social security/health position? Have you checked with relevant offices for overseas advice?

3. Do you know what you will do with your property?

4. Have you arranged removals, travel and pets?

5. Have you considered all the implications for family members?

6. How much preparation have you done – language/cultural/ professional?

# 7

## Your New Environment

### PRACTICAL MATTERS

#### Registering at the embassy/consulate

Although it is not a legal requirement to register with your country's embassy or consulate, if you are going to spend any time abroad it is a good idea to do so. In the event of military action, natural disaster or other turmoil, the consular staff can get hold of you more easily and ensure your safety. Equally so, should family in the UK be trying to reach you in the case of an emergency, the process can be speeded up if your whereabouts are known. For a registration card you will be required to present your passport, fill in some forms and pay a small fee. In addition to this, consular staff can give you advice and information on applying for your residence permit, driving licence and give guidance on administrative matters. It is also where you can obtain advice on what to do if there is a death in the family, or if a seriously ill person needs urgent repatriation.

Like all government officials, the consular staff can often be pretty busy and may not always be the most welcoming of people. Be tolerant and patient!

#### Obtaining a residency permit

You do not need to apply for this before you enter an EU country, and if your stay is for less than three months (even if you will be working), or if you will be undertaking seasonal work which does not exceed eight months, you do not need a resident's permit. However, you will need either a temporary or permanent residency permit if your stay is for longer. Permits vary in category but all can be renewed and extended. Spouses of people going there to work also require a permit and children under 14 may have their names endorsed on their parents' permit.

In all cases you need to pay a visit to your nearest Foreigners Service – be prepared and take all the suggested paperwork listed below. But be warned, regulations may change and you should not expect to manage everything successfully in one visit (it never works that way in foreign officialdom). Allow plenty of time; bureaucracy is slow and queues are generally long.

### What you may need to obtain your residency permit
*As an employee:*

- 2 photocopies of each page of your passport
- 3–6 colour passport-size photos
- declaration from your school/organisation stating your contract details.

You may also require evidence of a health certificate.

Self-employed people need to provide details of their work or business. People of independent means (including the retired) need to produce evidence that they can support themselves and their dependants without state assistance.

*As a dependant:*
- 2 photocopies of each page of your passport
- 3–6 colour passport photos
- 2 copies of your marriage certificate (if appropriate)
- 2 copies of your spouse's residency permit, if already obtained
- 2 copies of a letter from your spouse's school/organisation, stating s/he has a contract to work
- 2 copies of a letter from your spouse stating s/he will be financially responsible for you.

For children you may also require two copies of their birth certificates.

Once you have filled in the relevant forms you will be given a receipt (keep this safe), and eventually you will be informed that your permit is ready to pick up. To collect it you need the receipt and a small fee.

Your residency permit will be your official ID card in many countries. You will be required to carry it with you at all times. Until you obtain one your passport is your only ID.

For residency in non-EU countries, you must get clear instructions on procedures from the relevant consulates/official bodies before you try to establish yourself as a resident. In some countries it will be nigh-on impossible. If you have been offered a job by a school, ask them if they can give you information from inside the country itself, particularly if other non-native teachers have successfully managed to set up their residency.

## Other matters

You will probably need to open a bank account, as most schools prefer to pay directly into an account. Ask at the school which bank they recommend, and how you go about facilitating an account. The school finance office should also guide you on acquiring a tax, or fiscal, number (many schools do this for you when setting up your new job, but you should always check with the authorities that you are properly registered). It is also worth, at an early stage, locating a doctor and/or health centre.

Rebecca Chapman in Austria writes: 'There's a lot of bureaucracy in Austria for those just arriving. It is necessary to register with the police, get a bank account – the reputable schools prefer to transfer money directly into bank accounts – not cash in hand! You should also get a tax number from the local finance office. New laws mean that English teachers qualify for health care (extremely good!) and contribute to the pension scheme – which is reciprocal with the UK. Teachers therefore have to pay social security contributions – which should be taken off at source – reputable schools will register you with the social services and you'll receive a social security card with a number. Because the schools register you and also have to pay part of the contributions for you, they are only allowed to take on EU citizens. Non-EU members will find it virtually impossible to get work without various visas and work permits – which are again, virtually impossible to get!'

## Accommodation and facilities

Some schools offer accommodation with particular jobs, and this should always be accepted to start with, however dismal the place may prove to be when you get there. At least it gives you a base from which to venture out and look for alternatives whilst you are in that hectic initial period of settling into new routines. Some teachers have actually found accommodation offered them by their school to be good quality, and worth holding on to. You must check thoroughly beforehand with the school what financial arrangement there is regarding accommodation – what might seem at first glance a generous offer may turn sour if you subsequently find you are having large amounts of rent deducted from your wages.

## Guest houses

If you have no fixed abode to head for, you will need to sort something out for when you arrive. It is always expensive when you do first get to another country, until you find your feet and locate the best deals for living and socialising, so prepare in advance financially, so that you have enough to cover a stay in a guest house if you have to. Once you have started to talk to teachers at the school, you may well find someone who needs a flat-share, or can put you on to reputable accommodation agencies, families offering a room, or can tell you where to advertise yourself for a place.

If you have just ventured abroad without a job to go to, you will need to be ready to stay in guest houses or hostels, again until you establish a position or private work. You may find accommodation, particularly flat-shares, advertised in places like university notice-boards, or at the English schools themselves. For good advice on temporary lodgings, consult the Rough Guide to the country you're visiting, or look in the appropriate Living and Working books by How To or Kuperard for further ideas.

## Home-making

Once you have found somewhere to deposit your baggage, and use as a base, take time to make it into as much of a home as you can. This will make you feel better when things seem hard work and lonely. The most dreary of flats can be brightened up with a few coloured rugs and throws, some pictures or local artefacts. Finding where all your local facilities are for home-making, shopping, then socialising, is part of the hectic start to your new life. Try not to see it as another chore – go for exploratory walks to get to know your neighbourhood. Find your nearest grocers and bakers, discover where the locals go; you could even hop on a couple of buses and see where you end up. Despite how busy those first few days and even weeks may be at the school, it pays to take time to explore, as the sooner you start to integrate into the local scene, the more relaxed you will feel about your new way of life.

## UK moves

If you are going to stay in another part of the UK for ELT work, you may be interested in the following fascinating Web sites, which tell you all kinds of information about the area you may be moving to:

- *www.multimap.com* – a free service on hundreds of places in the UK, down to individual neighbourhoods, and even streets, showing houses for sale and rent, local facilities, hotels, and tourist information.

- *www.foe.co.uk* – Friends of the Earth site, showing locations of pollution.

- *www.aeat.co.uk/netcen/airqual* – information on the quality of the air in different locations.

- *www.landmark-information.co.uk* – detailed information on the land and previous pollution of it, such as mining hazards.

- *www.dfee.gov.uk/perform.shtml* – up-to-date school performance tables.

- *www.knowhere.co.uk* – local community reports on the areas in which they live, rating the towns for good and bad points.


## CULTURAL DIFFERENCES

### Learning the language

As mentioned previously, it is really essential that you try and learn at least the basics of the local language before you go. Although you may be heading for a mainly ex-pat area, and many foreigners do speak very good English, you ought to be aware of what is going on around you. When you make the effort a whole new world opens up to you, from conversing simply about your purchases at the market, to understanding legal documents and socialising with new local friends.

Hopefully you will have taken my earlier advice and started some language-learning before you arrive. Once you get there, there are many other things you can do to continue the good work and gain confidence, either formally or for yourself.

- Enrol on a course at a UK language school or college – look in the *Yellow Pages* for details, or check at the school where you may be teaching.

- Look out for private lessons, or conversation exchanges advertised in papers, church and school newsletters, or even bars.

- Start to read in the language – begin with a magazine of some interest, or a general interest magazine. Keep your expectations low to start with – small paragraphs before double-page spreads.

- Watch TV – yes, it really *IS* good for you! You may find it very fast to start with, but you can at least get used to the sound of the language. Programmes with English subtitles can be useful, although they are not always totally accurate translations.

- Play local radio when you are at home.

Slowly but surely you will gain confidence if you try. Don't be afraid of making mistakes – the locals will help you if you make an effort. Don't end up as one of those ex-pats who live abroad for 20 years and never utter more than a couple of words of the local language – unfortunately they still do exist!

### Culture shock

Nicki Grihault, author of *Working in Asia* (In Print Publishing), defines culture shock as: 'simply the normal response to the combination of physiological and psychological stresses experienced in adjusting to an unfamiliar environment. It includes your horror at people eating fried grasshoppers on the streets of Bangkok, or bewilderment at African smiles that carry a thousand meanings, or headaches and sleep disturbance'.

A move to another country to work is difficult enough in terms of the practical aspects of shifting home and settling in to work and making new friends, without all the added pressures of a new culture, language, and sometimes hard-to-comprehend traditions. Some people manage it all very well, viewing it all as a wonderful opportunity to experience something totally different to what they have left behind. For the less gregarious, small differences may suddenly seem larger than life to cope with, and it's all part of the adapting process. Nicki reckons it 'takes about a year to reach "autonomy" when you can enjoy the positive aspects of the culture and accept the negative differences for what they are'. You may not have as long as that, in which case you need to think about your strategy for managing.

The Culture Shock! Guides are very useful in giving you an insight into foreign lifestyles and quirks. The following tips from Nicki Grihault are also worth thinking about:

- learn about your host country before you go
- take realistic expectations with you
- create a home as soon as possible
- keep busy and find friends
- don't blame all your problems on the place

- take it easy and keep healthy
- decide to enjoy the country
- don't forget your sense of humour.

## WORKING PRACTICES

The working day may be different from what you're used to, with shop opening hours different, and longer lunch times. At school you may find a different approach to the timetable, or working practices. You may find also, for example, that many more people than back home employ the services of a cleaning lady/daily help. It may be quite normal practice and even people of moderate means may do so.

Work, and social, etiquette has to be got used to and the only way to do it with any modicum of success is to throw yourself into taking on board how the locals live and behave. If you are shy, or reticent by nature, of course it's not going to be easy to start with. But in time, by going to places where you can meet locals (even if it's just a regular coffee at a certain café-bar), you'll begin to discover that you *can* integrate into the local lifestyle – if you allow yourself.

If you need the prop of the ex-pat community, find out where they hold events – the English papers abroad have listings, and schools, churches, bookshops often have details. Having access to fellow-compatriots can be reassuring and comforting, but rely on them too much and you will certainly miss out on much of what local society has to offer.

### At the school

All establishments have their own way of operating, however similar the product on offer actually is. You may have already gained some idea of what goes on through information sent to you in advance of your job. Otherwise, as soon as you can when you arrive, find out who everyone at the school is, particularly the people in positions of authority, or those who may prove helpful to you in case of problems. Try to get to know your fellow-teachers quickly as well, as they are an excellent source of information not only about how the school ticks, but about life in that town/country too.

Areas you may wish to enquire about could include:

- the facilities at the school and availability and access to them (and what people do in the event of break-down)

- what time do people tend to arrive at school – are there any meetings before classes? Are you expected to stay on afterwards?

- where all the books are and the school policy on following coursebooks – are students expected to provide their own, if not are they allowed to borrow them from school?

- what people do for lunch/coffee breaks, including the students themselves

- what paperwork has to be completed in relation to the classes registers/marked work/lesson plans/reports

- details about the classrooms and where your lessons will be held.


## HEALTH AND PERSONAL PROBLEMS

If you fall ill whilst you are away, you need to know what services and facilities are available to you to help. Depending on how serious your illness is, you should find out in advance:

- where local pharmacies are

- how to request supplies of medicines

- where the nearest doctor is and how you make an appointment; will you have to pay and which documents do you have to take along?

- are there any specialist medical services such as osteopathy, chiropodists, *etc.*?

- is there a dentist and optician?

- where is the nearest health clinic, and what facilities do they have there?

Not every overseas location will be able to boast all of these services, but in all but the most extreme cases you should be able to find the right service to overcome your problem.

When you arrive in a foreign town, on registering at the consulate ask their advice about local health services – they may have a list or be able to advise on facilities open to you. Make sure you know where the nearest chemists are to where you will be staying and near your place of work.

If you have a medical condition before you go abroad, make sure you have followed the advice on page 77, especially if your complaint allows you benefit payments of any kind.

## Sexual problems

It would be very short-sighted of anyone working and travelling overseas (or in fact anywhere) to think they can get away with having sexual encounters without taking precautions. In the UK condoms are available free of charge at health centres – you can pick up a small supply before you leave. They are on sale all over the world, so there should be no excuse for not using them. Some countries have a more relaxed approach to relationships than others – take care in your dealings of this nature. If you run into difficulties of a sexual type, advice should be available via the medical services or health centres, if there are any; however, for serious problems, such as the need for a termination of pregnancy, you may find that it is far more complicated to arrange for reasons of local culture or religion, and you may have to return home to sort things out.

## Personal problems

Sometimes the problems you experience are more of an emotional nature. Moving to a new country is a huge upheaval, and getting used to a totally new culture, way of living, a new workplace and colleagues, on top of carrying out the work itself, can all contribute to feelings of inadequacy and not being able to cope. Many people go through this, as well as missing family, friends and home comforts. It does take time to settle into new routines (whether overseas or just in another part of the UK), so prepare yourself mentally in advance:

- keep in touch with friends and family and get them to come and visit you

- get out and about in your local community – try to integrate into your new environment

- make friends with other teachers at the school, check out the social scene, or organise one yourself

- be nice to yourself – make time to relax with your favourite music, or do things that will have a positive effect like long walks, swimming, dancing – get those endorphins working on your mood

- have a supply of your favourite foods regularly sent to you (until you make the break and totally dive into local cuisine)

- remember that if the whole thing really does not work out, you're never *that* far from home; these days the world is smaller than it has ever been!

### Who can you talk to?

Colleagues at the school, flatsharers, phone-calls home – anyone with whom you feel you can get on and who will listen with sympathy, but also who will boost your spirits and push you in a more positive direction. If your problem is of a medical type, or perhaps sexual in nature, you may feel more comfortable talking with someone less familiar to you – does the school have a counsellor or a liaison officer for new employees? If not, ask at the local health centre/clinic for advice. Talk with other teachers, especially those who have been there for some time; they should be able to give you advice on the best facilities in the area. Chatting with other new recruits is also useful, as some of them could be going through similar emotional problems as yourself. You may be able to support each other, and once you've got over that hurdle, you will find things do improve.

## PROFESSIONAL PROBLEMS

What can you do if your problems are related to your work, the workplace, and people in that place?

### Your own work

If for some reason you feel your work is not going as you had hoped – overwhelmed by the amount, difficult students, lack of confidence in certain areas of instruction, not motivating or inspiring – you should have a chat with the Director of Studies or school manager.

If it is the amount of work that is causing you a problem, talk to other colleagues and compare your workload with theirs. How intense are their timetables? How do they allocate time for lesson preparation and follow-up marking or feedback to students? It could be that with all of the initial upheaval, you are feeling under par and not working to your usual capacity. You could try eating lots of fresh foods (if you can), drink lots of water, exercise and try to keep things in proportion. Organise your time efficiently, but realistically, and try to get into a regular pattern with your preparation work. If you feel you have been given too many lessons, ask if you could have a slightly reduced timetable until you adjust to your new environment.

Problem students can be reported and useful ways of dealing with them can be picked up in the staff room. Persistent troublemakers may be removed or transferred to another class.

If you feel your motivation or confidence need boosting, enquire about further training or staff development sessions. You may be able to follow an advanced formal training course at the school. Alternatively, there may be regular staff sessions where different teaching strategies are discussed. If these don't exist, have a word around the staff room, you may be able to persuade people to participate informally, even an hour in the local bar on a regular basis (which would also improve your social life to boot!).

## The workplace

Problems with your physical working environment may not be so easily remedied. You may come across examples such as:

- lack of materials/resources
- equipment that does not work
- heating – too much or too little
- cramped classrooms
- dingy atmosphere
- nowhere to keep you own things
- no facilities for food or drink
- bad lighting in entrance or on stairs
- no lift working and six flights of stairs to negotiate.

How could you solve these problems? What would *you* do to improve the above conditions?

Raising the problems in staff meetings (if there are any) may be useful. Be diplomatic if approaching school managers; if you appear to be too critical of the school you may be marked down as a potential troublemaker.

Some of the above problems could be solved quite easily, e.g. dingy rooms could be voluntarily painted, or posters put up. If you are genuinely concerned about safety or an aspect of public liability, you need to have a serious talk with the school manager (possibly with the backing of your colleagues). If nothing is done and you are still concerned, perhaps you should look around for a better option.

## Problem people

No one gets on with everyone else all of the time; we all have off-days and we all have preferences for the type of people we like to deal with in work and social situations. In smaller schools, particularly where you are likely to bump into most members of staff quite regularly, you may have to learn to tolerate a range of personalities. This does not mean you have to be best buddies with everyone in sight – but try to bite your tongue in difficult situations, and don't get drawn into dialogue which may result in ill-feeling. Walk away if necessary.

## Bullying

Bullying in the workplace is a growing problem, and often goes on in such insidious ways that it is not reported. It can take many forms, can be very subtle, but can really wear you down if you happen to be the recipient. If you think this is what you are being subjected to, talk to someone, don't suffer in silence. Remember too, that bullies are often insecure people who perhaps fear being usurped by new, talented members of staff. In many instances you can deflect their behaviour or attitude by getting them on your side (ask their advice about something), or simply by standing up to them. Show them that you won't stand for their nonsense and get on with your career. Not always the easiest of things to do if the bullying is coming from one of your important superiors. You may benefit beforehand from reading *Successful Assertiveness in a Week,* Dena Michelli (Hodder & Stoughton/Institute of Management 1998).

## Your superiors

So, if the problems are as a result of behaviour from your boss (senior teacher, school manager, Director of Studies), what can you do? The vital thing is not to keep it all to yourself. This will simply allow the situation to continue unfettered, and the stress you are experiencing will simply exacerbate and make you ill. Many people do fear exposing the untoward behaviour of their boss, as the implications may result in a sacking. But you have a right to speak out, for yourself and others who may otherwise subsequently suffer.

Confide in a colleague first, to share your anxiety. You may find that this is a usual routine of try-on, or show of strength with new recruits and there may be tested means of dealing with it. If there is no other person in a position of responsibility in the school to whom you can take your complaint, you will have to confront the person causing the problem. Be calm, and polite – and ask them to refrain from their behaviour as it is making your life uncomfortable and difficult. If reasoning does not work, you may want to go a step further and threaten with further action. If taking this stance, you would be advised to contact one of the ELT organisations to find out their take on the matter.

If nothing else works, you may be better off leaving the school but exposing the situation in a letter to ELT journals.

### Sexual harassment

If you truly believe you are being sexually harassed in some way, talk to someone immediately, whether you first confide in a friend or colleague, or go direct to the school manager. However small you think the problem is, do not let the situation continue. The school has an obligation to provide a safe working environment for its employees – tell them if this is not happening.

If your alleged incident is particularly serious you may wish to take the case further, involving disciplinary hearings or even the police, in which case you may do well to have the support of a friend.

If you think you need support in any of the above situations, read through How To's *Managing your Boss and Colleagues* and *Managing Difficult People*.

### CHECKLIST

1. Do you know where to register your presence in your chosen country?

2. Are you aware of how and where to get advice on the practical aspects of everyday life?

3. Have you thought about the different culture around you and considered how you might fit in?

4. What differences in working practices do you need to take on board?

5. Do you know where to turn for help with medical or personal problems?

6. How will you cope with problems in the workplace?

# 8

## Further TEFL Career Options

### EXTENDING YOUR CONTRACT

Your initial teaching contract is coming to an end. What are your thoughts on where you go from here? If you are at the start of your ELT career, chances are you will want to carry on with further teaching positions. You may wish to move on to another school/town/country, in which case you will be looking for work again in all the ways detailed in Chapter 4. But if you are happy where you are, you need to be discussing a renewal of your contract before you get to the end of your current work.

Arrange to see the Director of Studies, or school manager, to discuss your options. If they are as happy with you as you are with them, you could explore the possibilities for either different groups/types of courses, or more responsibility. Assess together how the first stint has gone and if there are areas that were particularly positive or negative for you. Perhaps you may be able to increase the hours you work, or offer yourself for particular courses coming up. What about your rate of pay? Is there leeway to negotiate a rise? (Compare what you have been receiving with colleagues, or in other schools nearby.)

Remember, renewing or extending a contract is a delicate operation of negotiation. Be firm, but polite, and be prepared to refer to all the good feedback (hopefully!) you have had. However, if the school holds a different view on your performance, or has less work coming up (typically in the UK there is much more demand in the summer or Easter), resign yourself to moving on. For people with some experience in ELT, you may wish to consider branching into related areas of work.

### WORKSHOPS/SUMMER COURSE LEADERSHIP

Many schools, particularly in the UK, run EFL workshops (for example over Easter), or summer schools, all of which are oriented by some sort of course leader. Summer schools can be frantic affairs, whether they are residential or not. From the smaller-scale, one-week one-group courses, to the full onslaught of a number of weeks hosting various-sized groups, with different ages and nationalities – all require the same level-headed and well-organised approach. Course leadership can often be split between the main administrative work required beforehand to set the whole thing up, and the actual overseeing of the running of the course for its duration. After the groups have departed there is also a lot of follow-up paperwork to complete.

## What qualities are needed for course leadership?
- Good organisation skills.
- Excellent people/communication skills.
- Versatility and flexibility.
- Lots of energy.
- Patience and diplomacy.
- A sense of humour.

## The job
Setting up a workshop or summer school begins a long way in advance of the event itself. Contacts are made with schools and agencies abroad who deal with visits overseas, and negotiations undertaken about types and numbers of groups, length of stay, accommodation and fees, amongst other things. Often schools have already built up a good working relationship with a number of overseas contacts, and may offer the same courses each year through these agencies. However, part of your job may be to work with other sections at the school to pursue new contacts.

The courses themselves have to be meticulously planned to allow the groups maximum exposure to language in class-time, but balanced with activities and trips if required. Younger learners in particular have to be very well looked after. If courses are residential, suitable premises for the course must be found, and for students staying with families that accommodation must also be found and vetted.

The financial side of things will be carefully monitored with those at the school holding the purse-strings: setting the fee for the course, how much host families will be paid, payments for premises, food and trips, paying wages for teachers and activity leaders, *etc.* Having a clear idea of figures will help. Finding personnel to work on the course (teachers, senior teachers, activity leaders, group leaders) is another important part of the job. You may transfer some of the school's regular teachers across to these special courses for their duration, or you may need to find additional outside expertise, through advertising or from on-spec applications. You will probably interview in conjunction with another member of the management team, but ultimately the hiring decisions could be yours, so would you know what to look for?

After the course, follow-up work must be carried out swiftly and efficiently: settling bills, checking the final accounts for the course, going through student feedback forms and any other feedback from people involved in all aspects of the course, and evaluating its success. Then the whole process starts again...

### The course

Once the course is underway, you may be responsible for situations such as those listed below:

- liaising with staff on-site in respect of the running of the course and activities
- family liaison – any problems from family or student need resolving with speed and tact
- checking arrangements for visits have been made (coaches, timetable, food, entry tickets...)
- overseeing the hiring of bicycles or other equipment for older students
- liaising with the leaders accompanying the groups from overseas – problems with discipline or student dissatisfaction with what they are receiving
- teacher satisfaction – are they being paid on time/do they have the resources they need?
- more serious problems, such as missing students, crime, or accidents.

In many of the above scenarios you will be supported by a hard-working team of course administrators, but you really do need to have your finger on the pulse all the time, and be able to keep calm.

These types of jobs can be found advertised in the national press, and ELT journals, or you may be able to apply internally at a school if a position comes up where you work.

## MANAGEMENT AND TEACHER-TRAINING

### Management

If you are planning to move into a management position, either within a small to medium-sized establishment, or by applying to one of the larger organisations, it will be necessary to evaluate how far you have come professionally, and what further steps you must take in terms of professional development.

You may find smaller schools willing to take people on into management without extensive business qualifications, although you will be expected to have some business knowledge in addition to a number of years' ELT experience. The larger chains and organisations do demand much more; for example, the British Council requires of its middle-management some business qualification or an MA related to the area, and at least five years' ELT work, some of which must have been abroad. Anyone progressing through to senior management positions should have an MA/MBA as well as extensive teaching and management experience gained overseas. English First, a large chain group with over 35 years' experience operating in EFL across the world offers good prospects for their Operations Managers. A typical advert from them will demand that potential candidates for such a position are:

- excellent people-managers
- amazing organisers with a keen eye for details
- incredible problem-solvers
- totally committed to customer service
- graduates with business experience
- fluent in the language of the country involved.

Tall order? If you think you fit their bill, you can contact them for general information on their operations at: EF International Language School, Kensington Cloisters, 5 Kensington Church Street, London W8 4LD. Tel: (020) 7795 6615. Email: siobhan.pitchfork@ef.com and Web sites *www.ef.com* and *www.englishtown.com*

There are various advanced qualifications you can take, including the MA programmes mentioned in Chapter 3. There is also a Diploma in Educational Management (ELT), specifically designed for potential EFL managers. It is offered as a distance-learning course by a number of organisations, including International House in London. The UCLES Advanced Diploma in Teaching Management is currently on hold. Diane Hughes from Lancaster recently took an MA in the Teaching of English for International Business, on offer at the University of Central Lancashire (Preston). There was extensive input from the School of Business, with a work placement, in Diane's case shadowing a manager in a chemicals company, which gave her an insight into the business side of affairs. She says this was extremely useful, not only in terms of the managerial side, but also for any future teaching of students from a strong business background. The course (and others like it) are usually offered as a one-year full-time course, although most people tend to take it part-time. Diane advises that it may be difficult to complete in just one year, as there is a heavy coursework element to it, but she recommends it as an alternative to an ELT Diploma.

## Teacher-training

Becoming a teacher-trainer is not the easiest of positions to move into, not least because you do need to have many years of teaching behind you first before you may be accepted as a trainer, as well as some idea of what training entails. And even if you have been a successful EFL teacher yourself, this does not mean you will make an ideal trainer; the switch from supporting student learning of communication skills to enabling a teacher to develop those skills is quite a difficult one. However, if this is an area you are interested in, you can start by offering yourself as a volunteer trainer – in the school where you already work. You may be able to work with some newly qualified or trainee teachers and see how that goes. The large EFL organisations, such as IATEFL, have Special Interest Groups for teacher-trainers; join them and get involved with their debates and workshops. You will find special stands at the annual conferences dedicated to those with an interest in this area. Sign up and get talking to people.

Once you have gained some experience you can put yourself forward for positions not only within the EFL school world, but also to programmes around the world looking for trainers in primary and secondary education. The VSO, for example, often requires people with this kind of background to help run programmes in needy countries, desperate to develop their own educational systems.

## EXAMINATION WORK

Many people find interesting short- and longer-term work with the

Exam Boards offering EFL examinations. The main board, UCLES, provides the very popular tests for learners of English, such as the Cambridge First Certificate, amongst others. The other awarding bodies are: AQA (the Academic Qualifications Alliance), offering the NEAB University entrance test in ESOL, and the AEB Junior and Senior English tests; they also offer the Pitman's ESOL test under their City and Guild's arm. The third Board is the London Board, now known as Edexcel, and offering under its international arm 'London Examinations' a range of tests simply called for the moment London English Tests.

There is a variety of positions available throughout the process of setting up the exam papers, then the huge task of marking thousands of scripts each year. The following may give you an idea of positions likely to be on offer.

### Question paper setting

Teams of people write the exam papers, usually overseen by a team-leader, or Chief/Principal Examiner. Payment may be per question (such as in multiple-choice questions), or per section/whole exam paper. If you are interested in this kind of creative work, you will need to have access to various sources of stimulus material (newspapers, magazines, radio broadcasts), which may form the basis of a text. Additionally, you should be able to manipulate the materials to a level where they test the students according to the syllabus/course content they have been studying. That is not always easy. You have to be very disciplined and be able to submit your work to deadlines – missed deadlines could ultimately result in exam papers not being ready on time.

### Question paper checkers

Checkers, assessors, verifiers, moderators are all terms for those people employed to proofread the exam papers in draft form, and later on in the process. You will be checking the actual exercises, to see if they are at an appropriate level; the content to check it is suitable for the age groups; the timing – can the paper be completed in the specified time? On top of this comes the more general, albeit vital, proofreading for typing errors. If you have eagle-eyes for printed mistakes, and you have a thorough knowledge of what candidates should expect in the exam, this could be stimulating work.

## Question paper marking

Large numbers of teams of markers are drafted in each year to get through the thousands of exam scripts. Often marking is conducted over weekend sessions. Otherwise you may be sent scripts to your home to mark and return. Usually the marking process begins with an orientation day, when the Principal Examiners give you guidance on the standards they are looking for and how you should mark particular exercises which might not have a clear-cut answer. If you decide to earn some money at the peak exam times (usually summer for UK exams, and winter for exams overseas), you must be very organised, and be able to commit yourself time-wise over the period, including attendance at meetings and marking sessions. It goes without saying that as the work is of a confidential nature, you should have private space at home in which to work. Fees are usually paid per script marked, plus attendance fees for the meetings. This can be exciting work, although after hundreds of similar scripts you may feel disillusioned with the level of stimulation. It is too easy to offer to mark a high number of scripts, then be swamped by the deluge of packets through your letterbox. Make sure you have a clear run of time to cope.

For these kinds of positions you may be typically asked for a background of degree-level education, an EFL qualification, plus at least three years' teaching experience. Contact the various Awarding Bodies for further details (see contacts list for addresses).

## Work at the Exam Boards

Positions in EFL admin/production/research/training could be on offer at the Awarding Bodies, which may offer longer-term, more permanent work. Keep your eyes on the press, or approach the EFL sections of the Boards directly. For some of the positions you may be asked for advanced qualifications, such as an MA, but some of the work may be less demanding.

## EFL tests agents

Some work is available working as agents throughout the world, to promote and sell the EFL tests offered by the Boards. Applicants are generally people with ELT backgrounds, who speak good English and another language, and who also have some business experience.

## WRITING AND PUBLISHING

### Writing

The EFL publishing business is vast and, for some established writers, extremely lucrative. New coursebooks, support books, teaching packs, readers and associated products are constantly being churned out to keep up with increasing demands around the world for interesting and developing materials. If you think you have a leaning towards writing materials of some type or other (and let's face it, most teachers do spend an awful lot of their time making their own resources), how do you break into what might seem to be a closed-shop environment? All publishers are constantly on the look-out for new writers, either with new ideas for a publication, or to create something the publisher has already planned. People who have had teaching experience are valued, either as sole authors, or part of larger writing teams, as consultants as well as actual writers. The main EFL publishers in the UK are:

- Cambridge University Press (CUP)
- Oxford University Press (OUP)
- Penguin/Longman
- Heinemann ELT
- Dorling Kindersley Ltd
- HarperCollins Publishers Ltd

See also contacts list on page 188 for additional addresses.

If you are interested in writing materials, write to the EFL sections of the publishing houses on spec, enclosing a CV, and explaining what you have to offer them. They do receive many letters like this, and will initially probably put you on file, unless you have a particularly interesting idea they may wish to pursue. You may be cautious about sending them your ideas; many authors are, in case the editor simply gives the idea to one of their own established writers. But you have to take that risk, otherwise you might never get them to bite. Be prepared to write to as many publishers as you can find, and keep pestering them until you get a positive response. However, it is wise not to spend a long time working on a project and then trying to find a publisher for it – it is better to have some ideas and some drafted sample material, perhaps a chapter or a snippet from something that could be developed. In many cases ideas and material have to be changed according to the editor's vision.

**Fees**
If you are taken on as a writer, your fees can be paid in various ways.

- For producing something like a pack of materials, or for working as a consultant on a project, you will probably receive a one-off fee.

- As a main author, or contributing writer, you will most likely be offered an advance (an amount of money paid up front, usually partly when you sign the contract, and partly when you deliver the goods), which is subsequently deducted from your first royalty payment, plus a royalty fee for each copy of the book sold. Typically the level of royalty fee can range from around 8 to 15 per cent of the *net* sales of the product (i.e. it is not a percentage of the cover price of the book). In some cases this works out as little as 10 pence per copy sold, but if the product is a success, this can work out over time as quite a nice little earner.

Publishers are also always looking for people to act as 'Readers' – who comment on proposals and sample material, and proofreaders, who check the proofs before going to print.

If you are thinking of going into any of these areas, you would be advised to join the Society of Authors, who can offer advice on contracts and fees, run conferences and interest groups, and through whom you may make useful contacts. Send for details of membership to: 84 Drayton Gardens, London SW10 9SB. Tel: (020) 7373 6642. An invaluable investment is also the *Writers' and Artists' Yearbook*, which is updated annually. Not only does it contain solid advice on writing and associated publishing practices, but also information about your tax liability as a writer, and what to do in cases of copyright infringement. In addition to this, the main feature of the book is the enormous number of contact names and addresses for all types of publications and organisations relevant to the world of writing and publishing.

**Publishing**
Many people go into publishing either straight after obtaining a university degree, or after some years in teaching or other business positions. There are various positions open to you at a publishing house.

- Desk-editor – works very much on the manuscript, liaising with the authors, the production sections of the business, prepares the manuscript for the typesetters, and handles the day-to-day aspects of getting the material from a script to a finished book.

- Editor – usually a more senior version of the above, does a lot more work directly with the authors and has a hands-on approach with the work.

- Publisher – generally speaking, this is the person controlling the finances for projects, looking for potential writers, proposing projects to the editorial management board, and totally responsible for the whole section. A publisher may report to an Editorial Director or Senior Manager.

- Production controller – could have different titles, but the role is to work with the editors, but handling the active production process of moving the manuscript through to a finished book. They work closely with the typesetters and printers, and report back on any problems, be they of a financial nature (the price of paper for example) or of a practical sort.

- Marketing assistants/executives – working very much on the selling side of the business, people in the marketing sections take on board what the editor and authors see as the main features of a new publication, and work creatively on catalogues, promotional leaflets, and prepare the company reps for the hard task of selling.

- Reps – these are the people at the chalk-face of selling, either via the bookshops, or through exhibitions at conferences and in schools. A lot of travel is normally entailed, as well as hard work and dedication to the company cause.

## RUNNING YOUR OWN BUSINESS

If you feel you would like to branch out into running your own EFL business, there are various areas you could consider.

### Homestays

You may have been involved in hosting foreign students yourself, in conjunction with your local EFL school. Homestays is a step further, as students stay with a family but are also taught within the home. To get involved as a host for this you should not only be able to offer suitable accommodation, but be in a position to give formal teaching to your student, which means being suitably qualified. This

| | Morning | Afternoon | Evenings |
|---|---|---|---|
| Sunday | | Arrival | Dinner and evening with teacher and family |
| Monday to Thursday | 3 hours' tuition with Host Teacher | 2.5 hours' tuition with visiting teacher | Self-access study |
| Friday | 3 hours' tuition with Host Teacher | At leisure. Study time or excursion with teacher | Evening may include visits, social events, pub or cinema, etc. |
| Saturday | Free time | | |
| Sunday | Morning departure, or lunch provided for afternoon departures | | |

Fig. 7. Typical homestay timetable.

will involve a set number of lesson-hours per day, plus conversation throughout the rest of the time. For example, a typical 25-hour weekly programme offered by the Channel English Studies organisation is shown in Figure 7.

Obviously, you will not be able to participate in this kind of activity if you work full-time, or are always out doing your own thing.

Taking homestay further still, you may decide you could effectively organise this kind of business yourself. How do you go about it then?

- Get hold of brochures from other homestay organisations, to see what they offer.

- Participate yourself in a scheme if you can, to find out what is expected of the host.

- Plan out how you are going to run things – perhaps you can get advice from a local EFL school, and maybe you can work in collaboration with them.

- You will need to build up a network of contacts overseas who will be able to send students to you – use any contact you have to set the ball rolling – friends, colleagues working abroad may be able to act as agents for you.

- You also need to think about how you will find suitable families and your criteria for vetting them.

- Publicity – you can start by making your own leaflets on computer, but you will need to consider advertising in various publications, and even on the net.

- The financial side of things – how you set your fees, payments, keeping accounts, implications for tax and National Insurance, and aspects of insurance.

### Contacts
- **Channel English Studies** – contact Sarah Williams for further details, at 66 Eddington Lane, Herne Bay, Kent CT6 5TR. Tel: (01227) 375394/369587. Fax: (01227) 367586.
  Email: ChannEng@aol.com

- **Direct Learning** – contact Karin and Keri Roberts, 71 High Street, Saltford, Bath BS31 3EW. Tel/Fax: (01225) 872530.
  Email: dl@dirlearn.ndirect.co.uk
  Web site: *www.dirlearn.ndirect.co.uk*

- **Home End Farm** – contact Ms Sue Lim or Miss Jane Amphlett, Home End Farm, Cradley, Malvern, Worcs. WR13 5NW. Tel/Fax: (01886) 880240. Email: sue@english-for-children.co.uk
  Web site: *www.english-for-children.co.uk*

### Teaching agency
Another business venture you might consider, which does not require purpose-built premises, is to run an agency for teachers, should there be sufficient demand in your area. You can run this type of business from home, provided you have a good space for an office, plus somewhere suitable to talk to teachers and potential student clients.

The way an agency usually works is to have a number of teachers on the books who can offer different expertise (in EFL that could mean different age groups, specific areas of ELT such as Business English, or English for Academic Purposes, teaching different nationalities). Students will be matched to an appropriate teacher, according to their individual requirements. Normally teachers are not asked to pay a registration fee (although some agencies do charge), but a percentage of what they earn will go to the agency before the teacher receives payment. The student, on the other hand, generally pays a fee to register, and this is how the agency makes the most part of its income. If you would like to think about setting up an agency, you should consider questions such as:

- how will you get your teachers?
- how will you find your students?
- how and where will you advertise?
- how will you set your level of fees, and what will you pay your teachers?
- what accounting will be necessary, and will you do it yourself?
- what room is there for expansion?

You will need to check with your local tax office about the implications of running a business from home; this may also have an effect on your mortgage, as your lender may consider it proper to change the status of your property from purely residential, and subsequently impose a surcharge on your payments. You may also need to look into public liability insurance.

### Running a school
Setting up your own EFL school takes a lot more serious planning. If you have suitable premises which could be turned into a school (with classrooms, staff-room, office, eating and bathroom facilities), you have a huge advantage. Otherwise you must look into buying or leasing property for your purposes, which will require careful financial budgeting.

The premises is one side of the matter; finding personnel, students, planning courses, marketing and publicity, acquiring resources, meticulous budgeting, are all aspects of this kind of business you should cover in great detail.

John Priestley, who has run Impact 92 in Lancaster since the late 1980s, and has now expanded into the Nordic countries, gives the following pointers to would-be school owners:

- focus carefully on what your customers *REALLY* need
- remember your greatest assets are your people
- don't be afraid to have a shift in the paradigm you originally set down
- think hard about all the possible consequences of going into the business
- be creative, but don't reject tradition.

You may opt to go into business with a partner. This may help in terms of support for the hard work, or from a financial point of view, but you will need to make sure everything is legally written down so that no misunderstandings can arise over responsibility – financial or professional.

It is highly likely you will have to consider a bank loan to get you started. Tread cautiously and don't rush straight into the burden of a highly loaded repayment scheme. You may be eligible for a start-up grant for new businesses – contact your local Job Centre, or Employment Services.

You may have to start small and build your business up according to demand and your resources. Some schools are also available for sale as a going concern; you can find them advertised in the press and ELT journals. Companies also exist which deal exclusively with the buying and selling of ELT businesses, such as ELT Acquisitions, 5th Floor, 1 Malet Street, London WC1E 7JN. Tel: (020) 7431 5333. Email: chrisg@englishworldwide.com

If you have the finance available, buying a business could be a viable option as many of the abovementioned aspects will already have been established. However, scrutinise the accounts and the way things have been moving in that part of the country – what reason is there for its sale?

If you involve the whole family in this venture, remember that it will not be easy work; you will need to pull together in both positive and negative times, and be aware you are all working towards future benefits.

Useful general publications on this issue include: *Teach Yourself Setting up a Small Business* (1997) and How To Essentials guides to *Buying a Franchise (2000)* and *The Ultimate Business Plan (2000)*.

You should also join an organisation such as ABLS (Association of British English Language Schools) or IALC (the International Association of Language Colleges), which can offer support and contacts, as well as aiming to raise standards amongst EFL establishments by regular inspections and accreditation schemes.

You can get very useful financial advice about this type of business start-up from people like Terry Philips, an ELT consultant specialising in school management. He can be contacted by email: tphill@globalnet.co.uk

## CHECKLIST

1. Could you successfully negotiate an extension to your existing contract?

2. Have you the skills to manage a summer school, or Easter workshop?

3. Are you suitably qualified and experienced enough to progress into school management or teacher-training?

4. Have you tried the Exam Boards for short-term examining work?

5. Do you have the creativity and persistence to try authoring? Are you armed with the necessary information to contact relevant publishers?

6. Have you done sufficient planning for a business of your own?

# 9

# TEFL World-wide – an Overview

This chapter aims to give a general overview of the range of possibilities for ELT work in the major zones of the world. Addresses of useful organisations and selected schools feature in the next chapter.

## THE UK AND EUROPEAN UNION

The European Union legislation of free movement to its member-states citizens gives access to a range of jobs, although it can still be difficult to work in the state school sector, especially as the UK has no state-recognised TEFL qualification. You still need tax numbers and residency permits, but these should be relatively easy to process. (NB – different rules apply to non-EU citizens. The requirements of individual countries should be checked out.) Although Norway recently voted against joining the EU, it does in fact accept EU citizens looking for work on the same basis as the rest of the Union, although its EFL market is currently quite small. Some markets are now overflowing with native speakers in positions, such as Spain, Italy, and to some extent Portugal and Greece, but there is also a higher number of schools to try. It is worth looking outside capital cities, as there is great competition in the larger places. It is easier further afield, but this will depend very much on where you think you could live. There is a growing demand for more specialised ELT, particularly Business English, where it may be vital to have experience of commerce to secure the better jobs.

## THE REST OF EUROPE

Great opportunities are appearing at speed in the former Soviet Bloc countries, and countries aspiring to membership of the EU. These generally offer lower costs of living, but with salaries now rising in an attempt to attract good teachers away from other ELT hot-spots.

| | |
|---|---|
| UK | Lots of summer work/more difficult as a newly qualified teacher to get a permanent job unless in a school which does not require Diploma/ freelance possibilities |
| Ireland | Very seasonal/summer courses are a good bet |
| Austria | Knowledge of German a basic requirement/a lot of competition/summer camps and private work available |
| Belgium | Strong demand for languages/a lot of competition/young learner camps popular |
| Denmark | High unemployment rate/low prospects/need a good knowledge of Danish to work in public sector |
| Finland | Many opportunities across the age range/many young learner schools/possibilities for less qualified teachers |
| France | Great demand for Business English/many private schools/abundance of freelance teachers in Paris |
| Germany | Great demand in Adult Education and community colleges/Business English important but usually require commercial expertise/need to know German |
| Greece | Huge demand/ approx 5,000 private schools/ less competition in the winter |
| Italy | Demand continues but harder to find work in the main cities/ opportunity to unofficially work freelance |
| Luxembourg | Very few opportunities for ELT work |
| Netherlands | Mostly Business English/high levels of fluency/ large dependency on freelancers |
| Portugal | Many opportunities, particularly with young learners/a lot of overseas recruitment/Business English very lucrative |
| Spain | Young learner market big/less opportunities for unqualified/private work and in-house well paid |
| Sweden | Public university network offers some positions/ Business English in demand/useful to have contacts and speak Swedish |

Fig. 8. Opportunities in the UK and European Union.

| Country | Prospects | £ earning rate | Cost of living | Bureaucracy |
|---------|-----------|----------------|----------------|-------------|
| UK | Excellent | ££–£££ | Variable | Smooth |
| Ireland | Poor | £ | High | Smooth |
| Austria | Fair | ££–£££ | High | Fair |
| Belgium | Fair | £–££ | High | Smooth |
| Denmark | Poor | £££/50% tax | High | Fair |
| Finland | Good | £–££ | High | Smooth |
| France | Good/excell. | £–££ | Reasonable | Fair |
| Germany | Excellent | £–£££ | High | Smooth |
| Greece | Excellent | £–££ | Cheap | Fair |
| Italy | Good | £–££ | Reasonable | Fair |
| Netherlands | Fair | £–£££ | High | Fair |
| Portugal | Excellent | £ | Reasonable | Smooth |
| Spain | Good | £–£££ | Reasonable | Smooth |
| Sweden | Fair | £ | High | Smooth |

Fig. 9. Comparison of earning rates and cost of living in the UK
and European Union.

However, it is becoming competitive as a result, and in some areas
conditions in the schools, and day-to-day living, are not ideal. A
number of voluntary and cultural organisations have growing links
in Central and Eastern Europe, with some placings available. Some
zones are still in volatile areas and are not yet stable enough to
support ELT, however, there is plenty of scope in the remaining
areas to make this one of the most widely-sought world ELT
destinations.

## SUB-SAHARAN AFRICA AND ASIA

- **Pacific Rim** – there have been many recent economic upheavals
  resulting in cut-backs and unemployment. However, companies
  particularly see the need for English in the global market, and

| | |
|---|---|
| Bulgaria | Quite a good ELT structure/heavy teaching loads/winter hardships |
| Croatia | English in demand as the economic situation improves/restrictions in state sector/some well-established private schools |
| Cyprus | Small number of private schools/strong policies on immigration/locals tend to get most work |
| Czech Republic | Huge demand/easy to freelance and opportunities for non-qualified/Prague more difficult |
| Estonia | Large number of universities and private schools/growing market/harsh winters |
| Georgia | Growing market/opportunities for non-qualified and on-spec applications/most work in the capital |
| Hungary | Great demand especially for native speakers/ work for unqualified/quality of schools varies a lot |
| Latvia | Growing demand/few private schools/low earnings/better in-house and freelance |
| Lithuania | Few opportunities for non-experienced/currency problems/Ministry of Education offers posts |
| Poland | Many opportunities in all sectors/ private teaching good/useful to know Polish |
| Romania | Still behind other markets/ poorly equipped schools/low wages and high rent |
| Russia | Expanding market/ opportunities for unqualified/ General English important, with Business English growing |
| Slovak Republic | Slower growth than Czech Rep./state sector difficult/ private teaching, particularly for exam preparation |
| Slovenia | Well-established markets/easy to freelance/ General and Business English |
| Switzerland | Great demand for Business and General English/qualified teachers particularly required/ opportunities for holiday work |
| Turkey | Increasing demand/often attractive packages offered/freelance illegal but happens/areas of conflict |
| Ukraine | High demand/lack of teachers at all levels/state sector not possible, but university posts available |

Fig. 10. Opportunities in the rest of Europe.

| Country | Prospects | £ earning rate | Cost of living | Bureaucracy |
|---|---|---|---|---|
| Bulgaria | Good | £ | Cheap | Fair |
| Croatia | Excellent | £ | Cheap | Fair |
| Cyprus | Poor | £ | Cheap | Difficult |
| Czech Rep. | Excellent | £ | Reasonable | Fair |
| Estonia | Good | £ | Cheap | Fair |
| Georgia | Good | £ | Cheap | Smooth |
| Hungary | Excellent | £ | Cheap | Fair |
| Latvia | Fair | £ | Reasonable | Smooth |
| Lithuania | Poor | £ | Reasonable | Fair |
| Poland | Excellent | £ | Cheap | Fair |
| Romania | Poor | £ | Cheap | Difficult |
| Russia | Good | £–££ | Reasonable | Difficult |
| Slovak Rep. | Good | £ | Cheap | Fair |
| Slovenia | Good | £ | Cheap | Fair |
| Switzerland | Fair | £££ | High | Fair |
| Turkey | Excellent | £–£££ | Reasonable | Difficult |
| Ukraine | Excellent | £–££ | Cheap | Difficult |

Fig. 11. Comparison of earning rates
and cost of living in the rest of Europe.

local economies can probably continue to sustain demand. This year the Hong Kong government launched its Workplace English Campaign, encouraging companies to ensure employees are up to an adequate level of fluency. Huge amounts of money have been pledged to support the movement. There is growing competition from Australian teachers searching for work.

- **The rest of Asia** – here there are far fewer private schools and less opportunities, as many countries are a lot poorer. There is more scope for voluntary work and participation in teacher-training schemes.

● **Sub-Saharan Africa** – many countries here have English as an
official language, therefore providing few opportunities outside
the state sector. Those countries needing EFL teachers are not
able to support them financially and so rely on volunteer
organisations. The exception is South Africa.

## THE AMERICAS

● **Latin America and Caribbean** – Despite ever-shifting economies
in this part of the world, and in some areas a lack of financial
support for overseas expertise, Latin America still remains a
world area attractive to ELT teachers. Although strong
economic ties with the USA lead to a predominant desire to
learn American English, nevertheless, there are opportunities for
teachers from a non-USA background. In many countries, but
particularly Brazil, the network of Cultura Inglesa schools,
which are considered prime locations not only to learn English,
but also to teach, ensure a sufficient number of possible
positions. In other countries on this vast continent, jobs may
only be a reality via the aid agencies and voluntary work. A
recent research project undertaken for the British Council has
resulted in a huge publication that should be available for
consultation in libraries. EMLA (English Markets Latin
America) assesses the market opportunities throughout the
region. Further information from: The English Company (UK)
Ltd, 2 Western Rd, Wolverton, Milton Keynes MK12 5AF. Tel:
(01908) 220183. Fax: (01908) 220447. Web site: *www.english.co.uk*

● **USA and Canada** – Generally speaking, it is quite difficult for
non-native Americans to find ELT work in the States, apart from
in some of the smaller schools and training centres. However, in
Canada the story is very different, and an increasing demand for
English from its French-speaking citizens plus a rising number
of immigrants, means there are likely to be openings,
particularly for private and in-house work.

## NORTH AFRICA AND THE MIDDLE EAST

There are a small number of positions in North Africa, but the
really lucrative deals come from the oil-rich Gulf States, where
extremely attractive packages can be negotiated. However, the whole

| Australia | Huge growth from overseas students/overseas qualifications need to be assessed for equivalence |
|---|---|
| New Zealand | Seasonal demand/qualified native or fluent speakers welcomed/Auckland best place |
| Brunei | Strict qualification regulations/need driving licence/CfBT main recruiter |
| Cambodia | English still in demand/some instability/casual work easy to find |
| China | Huge demand especially in the growing commercial sector/emphasis on having a university degree/VSO also recruit |
| Hong Kong | Continuing demand/opportunities in all sectors/non-qualified freelancers will find work |
| Indonesia | Great economic and political instability/increased EFL market/large number of language schools |
| Japan | Many opportunities for non-qualified giving conversation classes/exchange schemes/on-spec positions/outside Tokyo less competition |
| Malaysia | Often ask for degree and 3 years' experience/suffering economy/part-time and private work |
| Myanamar (Burma) | Difficult political situation/private education not deemed legal, but tolerated |
| Singapore | Particular demand from young learners and for Business English/freelance work only with work permit/state posts via Ministry of Education |
| South Korea | A major destination for ELT work/harsh regulations on work permits/a lot of competition |
| Taiwan | Good demand even for minimally qualified/summer school season good/preference for N. American teachers |
| Thailand | High demand but many posts taken by travellers/hard to get good, well-paid work/March and May holidays best |
| Bangladesh | Most teachers need to fund themselves/some part-time work taken mostly by ex-pats/teacher-training opportunities |
| India | Increasing demand but few opportunities in private sector/unpaid work in state sector possible/some private English-medium schools |
| Nepal | Kathmandu best possibilities/poor wages and resources in many schools/a lot of voluntary work |
| Sri Lanka | Unpredictable situation/English being developed more/no work on spec |
| South Africa | Fast-growing market/S. Africans get the jobs first/Cape Town and Johannesburg best places |

Fig. 12. Opportunities in Sub-Saharan Africa and Asia.

| Country | Prospects | £ earning rate | Cost of living | Bureaucracy |
|---|---|---|---|---|
| Australia | Excellent | ££–£££ | Reasonable | Fair |
| New Zealand | Good | £ | Reasonable | Difficult |
| Brunei | Poor | £–£££ | High | Difficult |
| Cambodia | Fair | £–££ | Cheap | Fair |
| China | Excellent | £ | Cheap | Difficult |
| Hong Kong | Excellent | ££–£££ | High | Difficult |
| Indonesia | Good | £ | Very cheap | Difficult |
| Japan | Excellent | £–£££ | High | Fair |
| Malaysia | Fair | £ | Cheap | Difficult |
| Myanmar | Poor | £–££ | Very cheap | Fair |
| Singapore | Fair | £–££ | Reasonable | Fair |
| South Korea | Good | £–£££ | Cheap | Difficult |
| Taiwan | Good | £–£££ | High | Difficult |
| Thailand | Poor | £ | Cheap | Difficult |
| Bangladesh | Poor | £ | Very cheap | Difficult |
| India | Poor | £ | Very cheap | Difficult |
| Nepal | Poor | £ | Very cheap | Fair |
| Sri Lanka | Poor | £ | Cheap | Fair |
| South Africa | Fair | £ | Reasonable | Fair |

Fig. 13. Comparison of earning rates and cost of living
in Sub-Saharan Africa and Asia.

of this part of the world continues to be potentially volatile, and
certain zones are to be avoided – the Foreign Office always issues up-
to-date warnings about countries and you would be advised to check
with them first. There is also the problem of culture differences, and
women, particularly, may find many avenues closed to them.
Partners of ex-pats working in the Gulf may find some work
teaching privately, particularly younger learners.

| Argentina | Increasing demand, but growing competition for work/ private teaching not difficult/British Council has list of schools and Cultura centres |
| --- | --- |
| Bolivia | Has undergone economic problems and has not emerged unscathed/some demand for English/very low cost of living attracts some travelling workers |
| Brazil | Large market for young learners, including private work/large number of schools, but vary in quality/all-year possibilities on spec |
| Chile | The country is recovering after its decline of 20 years ago/many opportunities for in-house work as foreign investment continues to improve/hard competition from well-trained locals |
| Colombia | Growing demand, especially from companies/ larger cities have most possibilities/easy to find work even for unqualified |
| Costa Rica | A safe destination/many schools but not all have proper facilities/knowledge of Spanish improves possibilities |
| Cuba | Suffering economic difficulties/growing tourist industry/ demand for English may increase |
| Ecuador | Huge number of private schools/business and young learners, with General English very popular/easy to find work, even for unqualified |
| Guatemala | Fair demand/many USA teachers/limited number of private schools |
| Jamaica | Small amount of work available, including work with students struggling with English at school/exchange student schemes widely used |
| Mexico | Good demand particularly from companies/university degrees accepted but better work with teaching certificates/Business English the main market |
| Peru | Growth in economy and demand for English/General, Business and ESP/private tuition possible but work permits required |
| Uruguay | Some demand, now growing/most positions in young learners bilingual schools/work possible if unqualified |
| Venezuela | Inflation high so possible implications for wage rates/ some smaller schools offer work whether qualified or not/British Council can offer work |
| USA | Adults and young learners large markets/often need at least an MA/lower level of qualification demanded at trade and training schools |
| Canada | Increasing demand/private sector growing quickly/little work in Quebec |

Fig. 14. Opportunities in the Americas.

| Country | Prospects | £ earning rate | Cost of living | Bureaucracy |
|---------|-----------|----------------|----------------|-------------|
| Argentina | Good | £–£££ | High | Fair |
| Bolivia | Fair | £ | Very cheap | Smooth |
| Brazil | Excellent | £–£££ | Reasonable | Difficult |
| Chile | Good | £ | Cheap | Fair |
| Colombia | Excellent | £–£££ | Reasonable | Difficult |
| Costa Rica | Fair | £ | High | Difficult |
| Cuba | Poor | £ | High | Difficult |
| Ecuador | Excellent | £ | Cheap | Difficult |
| Guatemala | Fair | £ | Reasonable | Difficult |
| Jamaica | Poor | £–££ | Reasonable | Fair |
| Mexico | Good | £ | Cheap-ish | Difficult |
| Peru | Fair | £–££ | High | Difficult |
| Uruguay | Fair | £ | Reasonable | Fair |
| Venezuela | Fair | £ | High | Difficult |
| USA | Excellent | £–£££ | Reasonable | Difficult |
| Canada | Excellent | £–££ | High-ish | Difficult |

Fig. 15. Comparison of earning rates and cost of living
in the Americas.

| Bahrain | Little chance of on-spec work/qualified teachers only/fair attitude to women |
|---------|------------------------------------------------------------------------------|
| Egypt | Better schools require minimal qualifications/ potential work with oil companies/some work possible in international-type schools |
| Israel | British Council has main centres in Tel Aviv, Jerusalem, Nazareth/voluntary work possible, but potential danger zones/little real demand |
| Jordan | Main market is for younger learners/difficult to find full-time work on spec/increasing demand |
| Kuwait | Hard to find work without qualifications/ possibilities for private work/EFL industry finding its feet again |
| Morocco | Increasing popularity for English/mostly young learners and company work/good to know French |
| Oman | More laid-back country, with opportunities for women/CfBT have positions/not as lucrative as other Gulf States |
| Saudi Arabia | English increasingly used in commerce/most work in-house company training sections/private classes mostly taken by partners of ex-pats |
| Syria | Most work available to qualified teachers/British Council demands certificate even for part-time work/demand is generally quite high |
| Tunisia | Increasing use of English in commerce is creating more ELT possibilities/generally, though, not a large demand/Arabic or French a good skill |
| United Arab Emirates (UAE) | Good packages available/generally positive demand, especially for part-time/qualified teachers stand excellent chance of work |
| Yemen | Little internal financial support for EFL/number of private schools using English as medium for the curriculum is on the increase/oil companies provide most of the best positions |

Fig. 16. Opportunities in North Africa and the Middle East.

| Country | Prospects | £ earning rate | Cost of living | Bureaucracy |
|---|---|---|---|---|
| Bahrain | Fair | ££ | High | Fair |
| Egypt | Fair | £–££ | Cheap | Smooth |
| Israel | Poor | ££ | High | Difficult |
| Jordan | Fair | ££–£££ | High-ish | Fair |
| Kuwait | Fair | £–£££ | High | Difficult |
| Morocco | Good | £ | Cheap | Fair |
| Oman | Fair | £–££ | High-ish | Difficult |
| Saudi Arabia | Good | ££–£££ | Reasonable | Fair |
| Syria | Poor | £ | Cheap | Fair |
| Tunisia | Poor | £ | Reasonable | Difficult |
| UAE | Good | ££ | Cheap-ish | Difficult |
| Yemen | Good | £ | Very cheap | Fair |

Fig. 17. Comparison of earning rates and cost of living in
North Africa and the Middle East.

# 10

## Country Information A–Z

This chapter looks at a number of countries world-wide, listing useful addresses of British Council offices, embassies and consulates, and a selection of chain-school groups and other main teaching contacts. These details should kick-start your search for work. For a more detailed listing, see the *EL Teaching Guide* (*EL Gazette*, annual publication) and *Teaching English Abroad* (Vacation Work 1997), plus look out for contact information in ELT journals.

### ARGENTINA

**Embassy** – 65 Brook Street, London W1Y 1YE. Tel: (020) 7318 1300
**British Council** – Marcelo T de Alvera 590, 4th Floor, 1058 Buenos Aires
**Ministry of Education** – Pizzurno 935, 1020 Buenos Aires
**International House** – IH Belgrano, Arcos 1830, 1428 Capital Federal, Buenos Aires.
IH, JA Pachecho de Melo 255, (1425) Capital Federal, Buenos Aires
IH Cosme Beccar 225, (1642) San Isidro, Provincia de Buenos Aires.

### Other school contacts

- Asociación Argentina de Cultura Inglesa, Suipacha 1333, (1011) Buenos Aires
- CAIT (Capacitación en Idiomas y Traducciones), Av. Pte. Roque Saenz Pena 615, Piso 6, 1393 Buenos Aires. Email: cait@ciudad.com.ar
- Instituto Cultural Argentino-Britanico, Calle 12, No 1900, La Plata
- ITESL Foundation, Malaver 1586-PC (1602) Florida, Buenos Aires
- Asociación Argentina de Cultura Britanica, Av. Hipólito Yrigoyen 496, Córdoba. Email: aacb-cba@satlink.com
- St Johns School, Recta Martinoli 3452, V Belgrano 5417 Córdoba, Pica de Córdoba

## AUSTRALIA

**High Commission** – Australia House, Strand, London WC2B 4LA. Tel: (020) 7379 4334

**British Council** – Edgecliff Centre, 401/203 New South Head Road, PO Box 88, Edgecliff, Sydney NSW 2027

**Australia TESOL** – PO Box 296, Rozelle, New South Wales 2039

**International House** – IH Queensland, Box 7368, Cairns Mail Centre, QLD 4870

IH Sydney, City Campus, Waratah Education Centre, 22 Darley Road, Manly, NSW 2095

**EF English First** – EF International Language Schools, Ground Floor, 5–7 Young Street, Sydney, NSW 2000

### Other school contacts

- AG Mate Academy, Level 12, 33 Bligh Street, Sydney NSW 2000
- Adelaide, University of South Australia, SA 5005
- Australia World College, PO Box 36, Katoomba NSW 2780
- Australian College of English, PO Box 82, Bondi Junction, Sydney NSW 2022
- Australian Premiere College, PO Box 1234, Strathfield NSW 2135
- Billy Blue English School, PO Box 728, 124 Walker Street, North Sydney NSW 2059

## AUSTRIA

**Embassy** – 18 Belgrave Mews West, London SW1X 5HU. Tel: (020) 7235 3731

**British Council** – Schenkenstrasse 4, A-1010 Wien Tel: (1) 533 2616-80

**Ministry of Education** – Minoritenplatz 5, A-1014 Vienna

**The Austrian Institute** – 28 Rutland Gate, London SW7 1PQ.

**TEA** – Teachers of English in Austria, TEA Office, Kleine Neugasse 7/2a, A-1050 Vienna

**International House** – IH Schwedenplatz 2/55, 1010 Vienna

**inLingua** – iL, Rechbauerstr 23/2, A-8010 Graz

iL, Sudtiroler Platz 8/2, A-6020 Innsbruck

iL, Landstrasse 24, (Ecke Spittelwiese), A-4020 Linz

**Berlitz** – Berlitz Sprachschule, Rotenturmstrasse 1–38, 1060 Vienna

## Other school contacts

- Austro-British Society, Wickenburgasse 19, 1080 Vienna
- English Language Centre, In der Hagenau 7, 1130 Vienna
- Innsbruck International Highschool, Schonbeg 26, A-6141 Innsbruck
- Mini Schools and English Language Day Camp, Postfach 160, 1220 Vienna
- Sprachinstitut, Florianigasse 55, 1080 Vienna
- Berufsforderungsinstitut, Kinderspitalgasse 5, 1090 Vienna

## BAHRAIN

**Embassy** – 98 Gloucester Road, London SW7 4AU. Tel: (020) 7370 5132

**British Council** – AMA Centre, 146 Sheikh Salman Highway, PO Box 452, Manama 356. Tel: 261555

**Ministry of Education** – PO Box 43, Isa Town

## Other school contacts

- Al Rawasi Academy, Mina Salman, Bahrain
- Child Development, PO Box 20284, Manama
- Polyglot School, PO Box 596, Manama
- The Cambridge School of English, PO Box 20646, Manama
- Gulf School of Languages, PO Box 20236, Manama
- Bahrain Computer and Management Institute, PO Box 26176, Manama

## BELGIUM

**Embassy** – 103 Eaton Square, London SW1 9AB. Tel: (020) 7470 3700

**British Council** – Britannia House, 30 rue Joseph 11, 1040 Brussels. Tel: (2) 219 3600

**Ministry of Education** – (Flemish) Centre Arts Lux, 4th & 5th Floors, 58 avenue des Arts, BP5, 1040 Brussels. / (French) 68a rue du Commerce, 1040 Brussels

**inLingua** – iL Antwerpen, Frankrijklei 39, B-2000 Antwerpen

iL Gent, UCO Building – 6de Verdieping, Bellevue 9/10, 9050 Gent (Lederberg)

**Berlitz** – Avenue de Tervuren 265, 1150 Brussels

Avenue des Arts 36, 1040 Brussels

Rue du Pont d'Avroy, 2/4, 4000 Liege

**Other school contacts**
- Access BVBA Taalbureau, Abdijstraat 40, 2260 Tongerlo
- Bilingua, rue Renier Chalon 6, 1060 Brussels
- Kamer voor Handel & Nijverheid, VUB, Room 3B/208, Pleinlaan 2, 1050 Brussels
- Antwerpse Talenakademie, Karei Govaerstraat 23/25, 2100 Deume
- British Commission, rue de la Charité 39, 1040 Brussels
- May International, rue Lesbroussart 40, 1050 Brussels

## BRAZIL

**Embassy** – 32 Green Street, London W1Y 3FD. Tel: (020) 7499 0877
**Consulate** – 6 St Albans Street, London SW1Y 4SG. Tel: (020) 7930 9055
**British Council** – SCRN 708/9, Bloco F Nos 1/3, (Caixa Postal 6104), 70 740 Brasilia DF. Tel: (61) 272 3060
Av. Domingos Ferreira 4150, Boa Viagem (Caixa Postal 4079), 51021 Recife. Tel: (81) 326 6640
Rua Elmano Cardim 10, Urca, (Caixa Postal 2237), 22291 Rio de Janeiro RJ. Tel: (21) 295 7782
Rua Maranhão 416, Higienópolis, 01240 São Paulo SP. Tel: (11) 826 4455
**Ministry of Education** – Esplanada dos Ministérios, Bloco L, 70444 Brasilia
**BATE (British Association for Teacher Education)** – Rua Vinicius de Moraes 179, Ipanema 22411, Rio.
**LAURELS (Latin American Union of Registered English Language Schools)** – c/o International House, Rua 4, No 80, Setor Oeste, Goiania GO 74110-140. Tel: (62) 224 0478.
**International House** – IH Goiania, see above
Britanic IH Recife, Rua Hermogenes de Norais 163, Madalena 50 610–160, Recife PE.
**inLingua** – Rua Primeiro de Março 23-2 andar, Centro, 20010-000 Rio de Janeiro RJ
**Berlitz** – Berlitz Escola de Idiomas, Av.Presidente Vargas 435 – S/ loja, 20071 003 Rio, RJ.

## Other school contacts

- Associação Laumni (ALUMNI), Rua Visconde de Nacar 86, Real Parque Morumbi, 05685–903 São Paulo SP.
- Britannia Executive School, Rua Barão de Lucena 61, Botofogo, Rio de Janeiro 22260
- Centro Britanico, Rua João Ramalho 344, São Paulo SP 05008–011
- English Forever, Rua Rio Grande do Sul 356, Pituba, Salvador BA 41830–140
- Instituto de Língua Inglesa, Av.do CPA 157, Cuiaba MT 78008–000
- Sociedade Brasileira de Cultura Inglesa, Rua Fernandes Tourinho 538, Savassi BH, MG 30112–000. (Runs a huge chain group of Cultura Inglesa schools across Brazil)

## BULGARIA

**Embassy** – 186 Queens Gate, London SW7 5HL. Tel: (020) 7584 9400

**British Council** – 7 Tulovo Street, 1504 Sofia. Tel: 463346

**Ministry of National Education** – Blvd Knjaz Donkukov 2A, 1000 Sofia

## Other school contacts

- Alliance Centre for Teaching of Foreign Languages, 3 Slaveikov Square, 1000 Sofia.
- Business Private High School, Kosta Lulchev Street, Sofia
- First Private English Language Medium School, Stara Planina Street, Sofia
- Meridian, Macedonia Boulevard, Sofia 1606
- Avo-3 School of English, House of Culture Sredets, 2a Krakra Street, Sofia
- English Language Club, 143 Kniaz Boris 1 St, Entr 2, Sofia

## CANADA

**TESL Canada** – PO Box 44105, Burnaby, BC V5B 4Y2

**PELSA (Private English Language School Assoc.)** – c/o Pacific Language Institute, 3rd Floor, 755 Burrard St, Vancouver, BC, V6Z 1X6

**Canadian Council of Second Languages** – 151 Slater St, Ottawa, Ontario, T1P

**Berlitz** – 130 Bloor St West, Suite 603, Toronto, Ontario, M5S 1N5

### Other school contacts

- Academie Linguistique Internationale, 5115 Rue de Gaspe, Suite 300, Montreal, Quebec, H2T 3B7
- Brock University, Intensive English Language Program, Dept of Applied Language Studies, St Catherines, ON, L2S 3A1
- Canadian College of English Language, 1477 W Pender St, Vancouver, BC, V6G 2S6
- College of the North Atlantic, St Johns District, International Program Office, PO Box 1693, St Johns NF, A1C 5P7
- George Brown College, International Centre, PO Box 1015, St B, Toronto, ON, M5T 2T9
- International Language Institute, 5151 Terminal Rd, 8th Floor, Halifax, Nova Scotia, B3J 1A1

### CHILE

**Embassy** – 12 Devonshire Street, London W1N 2DS. Tel: (020) 7580 6392

**British Council** – Eliodoro Yañez 832, Casilla 115, Correo 55, Tajamar, Santiago. Tel: (2) 236-1199

**Ministry of Education** – Avenida Liberator B o'Higgins 1371, Santiago

**LABCI (Latin American-British Cultural Institutes)** – Instituto Chileno-Britanico de Cultura, Santa Lucia 124, Casilla 3900, Santiago

**Berlitz** – Av.Pedro de Valdivia 2005, Providencia, Santiago. Tel: (2) 204 4018

### Other school contacts

- Antofagasta British School, Pedro Leon Gallo 723, Casilla 1, Antofagasta
- Colegio Inglés de Talca, 12 Norte 5/6 Oriente, Talca.
- Instituto Chileno-Britanico de Cultura, Baquedano 351, Casilla 653, Arica
- International Preparatory School, Pastor Fernandez 16001, Al Arrayan, Santiago
- Redland School, Camino El Alba 11357, Las Condes, Santiago

- Wenlock School, Carlos Pena Otaegui 10880, La Foresta, Los Dominicos, Santiago

## CHINA (PEOPLE'S REPUBLIC)

**Embassy** – 49–51 Portland Place, London W1N 3AH. Tel: (020) 7636 5726

**Consular section** – 31 Portland Place, London W1N 3AG. Tel: (020) 7631 1430

**British Council** – Cultural and Education Section, 4th Floor, Landmark Building, 8 North Dongsanhuan Road, Chaoyang District, Beijing 100026. Tel: (1) 501 1903

**Education Commission** – 37 Damuchang Hutong, Xicheng District, Beijing

**State Bureau of Foreign Experts** – Friendship Hotel, 3 Bai Shi Qiao Rd, 100873 Beijing

**EF English First** – No 167 Taiyuan Road, Shanghai, PRC (2000031)

### Other school contacts

- Adult Education Training Dept, Beijing Normal University, 19 Xinjiekouwai, Haidian District, Beijing
- Beijing Overseas Applied Business Language School, Branch College of Dongchen Education College, 9 Donggong St, East Gulou St, Dongchen District, Beijing
- Changchun Kelian Foreign Languages Training Centre, 80 Tongzhi St, Changchun, Hilin (130021)
- EFT International Standard Degree Peiqing School, Xinzhonglie Primary School, opp. Zhonglie, Beijing.
- Modern International Languages Inst., 4th Floor, Training Centre Building of Beijing, Bureau of Labour, Xizhimen, Beijing.
- Shili School, Room 147, West Hall, Shuangyushu Youth Apartment, Haidian District, Beijing

## COLOMBIA

**Embassy** – 3 Hans Crescent, London SW1X 0LR. Tel: (020) 7589 9177

**Consulate** – 140 Park Lane, London W1Y 3DF. Tel: (020) 7493 4233

**British Council** – Calle 87 No 12-79, Apartado Aereo 089231, Santa Fé De Bogotá. Tel: (1) 218 7518

**Ministry of Education** – Centro Administrativo Nacional, 501 Avenida El Dorado, Bogotá
**Associación Colombiana de Professores de Lenguas** – Centro Oxford, Apartado Aereo 102420, Unicentro, Bogotá

### Other school contacts
- Academia Inglés para Niños, Calle 106 No 16–26, Bogotá
- Bi Cultural Institute, Avenida 7, No 123–97. Of. 202, Bogotá
- Centro Anglo Francés, Carrera 11, No 6–12, Neiva
- Centro Colombo Andino, Calle 19, No 3–16, Of. 203, Bogotá
- Centro de Lengua Inglesa, Calle 61, No 13–44. Of. 402, Bogotá
- Escuela de Inglés, Calle 53, No 38–25, Barranquilla

## CROATIA

**Embassy** – 18–21 Jermyn Street, London SW1Y 6HP. Tel: (020) 7434 2946
**British Council** – PO Box 55, 12/1 Ilica, 10000 Zagreb
**Ministry of Education** – Ave Vukovar 78, 10000 Zagreb

### Other school contacts
- Agencija F, Trg Frane Petrica 4, 51557 Cres.
- ELC-English Language Center, Kralja Tomislava 9, 40000 Cakovec
- Lancon, Kumiciceva 10, 10000 Zagreb
- Pucko Sveuciliste (Skola Stranih Jezika), L Jagera 6, 31000 Osijek
- Skola Stranih Jezika Ziger, Ivana Trankog 19, 42000 Varazdin
- Byron, Giardini 11, 52100 Pula

## CYPRUS

**High Commission** – 93 Park Street, London W1Y 4ET. Tel: (020) 7499 8272
**British Council** – 3 Museum Street, (PO Box 5654), 1097 Nicosia. Tel: (2) 44 21 52
**Ministry of Education** – Greg Axentiou Street, 1434 Nicosia
**Turkish Rep of N. Cyprus Office** – 28 Cockspur Street, London SW1. Tel: (020) 7837 4577

## Other school contacts

- AISC International School, 11 Kassos Street, Ay Omoloyitea, PO Box 3847, Nicosia
- Centre of Higher Studies, PO Box 545, 2 Evagorou Street, Floor 6, Nicosia
- Forum Language Centre, 47a Prodromou Street, Strovolos, Nicosia
- KES College, Kallipoleos Corner, Nicosia
- Massouras Private Institute, 1 Liperti Street, Flat 103, Paphos.
- St Johns School, BFPO 53, Episkopi

## CZECH REPUBLIC

**Embassy** – 26–30 Kensington Palace Gardens, London W8 4QY. Tel: (020) 7727 3966/7
**British Council** – Narodni 10, 12501 Prague 1. Tel: (2) 203751/5
**Ministry of Education** – Karmelitska 8, 118.12 Prague
**International House** – IH Lupacova 1, 130 00 Prague 3
**Berlitz** – Head Office Hybernska St 24, 110 00 Prague 1
Berlitz, Starobmenska 3, Brno
Berlitz, Jecna 3, 12, 120 00 Prague 2
**Linguarama** – Srobárova 1, 130 00 Prague 3

## Other school contacts

- Accent Language School, Bitovska 3, 140 000 Prague 4
- Akademie JAK, Nadrazni 120, 702 00 Moravska Ostrava
- The Bell School, Prague, Nedvezska 29, Prague 10
- The Caledonian School, Vitavska 24, 150 00 Prague 5
- D and D Jazykova Skola, Komenskeho 372, Modrice
- English Link, Na Berance 2, Prague 6

## DENMARK

**Royal Embassy** – 55 Sloane Street, London SW1X 9SR. Tel: (020) 7333 0200
**British Council** – Gammel Mont 12, DK-1117 Copenhagen K. Tel: 33 11 20 44
**Ministry of Education** – Frederiksholms Kanal 21–25, DK-1220 Copenhagen K
**EETAE (Association of English Teachers in Adult Education)** – Toftegardsvej, 24 DK 3500 Vaerlose

**inLingua** – European Education Centre Aps (Inlingua), Lyngbyvej 72, 2100 Copenhagen

**Berlitz** – Berlitz International, Vimmelskaftet 42a, 1161 Copenhagen

**Linguarama** – Hvilevej 7, 2900 Hellerup

## Other school contacts

- Access, Head Office – Hamerensgade 8, 1267 Copenhagen K
- Elite Sprogcentret, Hoffmeyersvej 19, 2000 Frederiksberg
- Activsprog, Head Office – Rosenvugets Alle 32, 2100 Copenhagen
- Erhvervs Orienterede Sprogkurser, Betulavej 25, 3200 Helsinge
- Babel Sprogtruning, Vordingborggrade 18, 2100 Copenhagen
- Frit Oplysningsforbund, Vestergrade 5000 Odense C


## ECUADOR

**Embassy** – 3 Hans Crescent, London SW1X 0LN. Tel: (020) 7534 1367

**British Council** – Av.Amazonas 1646, Orellana, Casilla 17 07 8829, Quito. Tel: (2) 540225

Costanera 504, Centre Las Monjas y Ebanos, PO Box 6547, Guayaquil. Tel: (4) 388560

**Ministry of Education** – Méjia 348, Quito

**Ecuadorian English Teachers Society** – PO Box 10935, Guayaquil

## Other school contacts

- International Benedict Schools of Languages, PO Box 09-01-8916, Guayaquil
- Benedict School, 9 de Octubre 1515, y Orellana, Quito
- Benedict School, Datiles y La Primera, CC Urdesa, Guayaquil
- Fulbright Commission, Almagro 961 y Colon, Quito
- ELC The Edinburgh Linguistic Center, Mariana de Jesus 910 y Amazonas, Quito, PO Box 17-21-0405, Quito. Email: juliovel@uio.satnet.net
- Experimento de Convivencia International del Ecuador, Les Embleton, Hernando de la Cruz 218 y Mariana de Jesus, Quito.


## EGYPT

**Embassy** – 2 Lowndes Street, London SW1X. Tel: (020) 7235 9719

**British Council** – 192 Sharia el Nil, Agouza, Cairo. Tel: (2) 345 3281-4

9 Batalsa St, Bab Sharki, Alexandria. Tel (3) 482 0199

**Ministry of Education** – 6 Amin Samy Street, El-Sayed El-Zeinab, Cairo

**Eygptian Education Bureau** – 4 Chesterfield Gardens, London W1Y 8BR

**International House** – International Language Institute (IH), 3 Mahmoud Azmy Street, Medinet El Sahfeyeen, Cairo

**Other school contacts**

- El Kawmeya International School, Horreya Avenue, Bab Sharki
- International Language Learning Institute, 34 Talaat Harb Street, 5th Floor, Cairo
- International Language Learning Institute, Pyramids Road, Guiz
- Victory College, Victoria Tram Station, Victoria
- El Manar School, Amin Fikry Street, Ramleh Station, Cairo
- El Pharaana School, El Phraana Street, Bab Sharki

## ESTONIA

**Embassy** – 16 Hyde Park Gate, London SW7 5DG. Tel: (020) 7589 3428

**British Council** – Resource Centre, Vani Posti 1, Tallinn 0001

**Ministry of Education** – Tönismägi 11, Takkinn 0106

**British Embassy** – Kentmanni 20, Tallinn 0100

**International House** IH Tallinn, Pikk 69, Tallinn EE0101

**Other school contacts**

- ALF Training Centre Ltd, Ravala pst 4, Tallinn EE0001
- Ko-Praktik, Tondi 1, Tallinn EE0013
- Old Town Language Centre (Helo), Puhavaimu 7, Tallinn EE0001
- Concordia International University, Kaluri tee 3, Viimsi veld, Harjumaa EE3006
- Kullerkupp, Parnu mnt 57, Tallinn EE0001
- Sugesto, Narva mnt 6-8, Tallinn EE0001

## FINLAND

**Embassy** – 38 Chesham Place, London SW1X 8HW. Tel: (020) 7235 9531

**British Council** – Hakaniemenkatu 2, 00530 Helsinki. Tel: (0) 701 8731

**Ministry of Education** – Rauhankatu 4, 00170 Helsinki 17

**ATEF (Association of Teachers of English in Finland)** – Rautatielai-senkatu 6A, 00520 Helsinki

**International House** – IH Habil Oy, Kieliopisto, Mariankatu 15B 7, 00170 Helsinki 17

**Berlitz** – Kaivokatu 10A, 00100 Helsinki

**Linguarama** – Linguarama Suomi, Annanakatu 26, 00100 Helsinki. Email: hki@linguarama.com

### Other school contacts

- AAC-Opisto, Kauppaneuvoksentie 8, 00200 Helsinki
- Lansi-Suomen Opisto, Loimijoentie 280, 32700 Huittinen
- Lingua-Forum Ky, Fredrikinkatu 61, A36, 00100 Helsinki
- Kielipiste Oy, Kaisaniemenkatu 4A, 00100 Helsinki
- IWG Kieli-Instituutti, Himeenkatu 25 B, 33200 Tampere
- The Federation of Finnish-British Societies, Puistokatu 1bA, 00140 Helsinki

### FRANCE

**Embassy** – 23 Cromwell Rd, London SW7 2EL. Tel: (020) 7838 2055. Web site: *www.francealacarte.org.uk*

**Consulate** – 6a Cromwell Rd, London SW7.

**British Council** – 9–11 rue de Constantine, 75007 Paris. Tel: (1) 45 55 95 95

**French Institute** – 14 Cromwell Place, London SW7 2JR. Tel: (020) 7581 2701

**Ministry of Education** – 110 rue de Grenelle, 75007 Paris

**FBCCI (Franco-British Chamber of Commerce and Industry)** – 41 rue de Turenne, 75003 Paris

**TESOL France** – 15 rue Daguerre, 92500 Ruell-Malmaison

**International House** – IH Centre d'Anglais d'Angers, 16 rue des Deux Haies, 49000 Angers

IH Centre de Langues Riviera, 62 rue Gioffredo, 06000 Nice

IH 152 Alles de Barcelona, 31000 Toulouse

**inLingua** – (amongst others) iL Aix-en-Provence, 115 rue Claude Nicolas Ledoux, F-13854 Aix-en-Provence CEDEX 03

iL Colmar, 12 rue Berthe Molly, F-68000 Colmar

iL Hazebrouck, 41 avenue du Marechal de Lattre de Tassigny, F-59190 Hazebrouck

**Linguarama** (amongst others) Dijon, Amphypolis, 10 rue Paul Verlaine, Rond point de l'Europe, 21000 Dijon
Grenoble, 6 rue Roland Garros, Mini parc Alpes Congres, 38320 Eybens
Lyon, Tour Credit Lyonnais, 129 rue Servient, 69003 Lyon

## Other school contacts
- Access Langue Speakwell, 35 rue de Ponthieu, 75008 Paris
- British Institute, 11 rue de Constantine, 75007 Paris.
- European Executive Services, 2–6 rue de Strasbourg, 93110 Rosny sous Bois
- ILC/International House, 20 Passage Dauphine, 27 rue Mazarine, 75006 Paris
- Isform Champs-Elysées, 19 rue de Berri, 75008 Paris
- Lingua Formation, 57 rue d'Amsterdam, 75008 Paris

## GEORGIA

**Embassy** – 3 Hornton Place, Kensington, London W8. Tel: (020) 7937 8233
**British Council** – 13 Chavcharaze Avenue, 2nd Floor, Tbilisi 380079
**Ministry of Education** – Uznadze 52, 38002, Tbilisi
**International House** – IH Tbilisi, 2 Dolidze St, Tbilisi 380015

## Other school contacts
- Centre for Applied Language Studies, International House, 26 May Square, 380015 Tbilisi
- International Language Academy, 17 Chavchavadze Avenue, Tbilisi 380079
- Public Service Language Centre, 8 Rustaveli Ave, Tbilisi
- Nike English and Computer Teaching Firm, 8 Jambuli St, Tbilisi 380008
- Byron School of Tbilisi, 2 Griboedov St, Tbilisi

## GERMANY

**Embassy** – 23 Belgrave Square, London SW1X 8PZ. Tel: (020) 7824 1300. Web site: *www.german-embassy.org.uk*
**Consulate General** – Westminster House, 11 Portland Street, Manchester M60 1HY. Tel: (0161) 237 5255
**British Council** – Hahnerstrasse 6, 5000 Cologne 1. Tel: (221) 20 64 40

Hardenbergstrasse 20, 1000 Berlin 12. Tel: (30) 31 10 99
Rothenbaumchaussee 34, 2000 Hamburg 13. Tel: (40) 4460 57
Lumumbastrasse 11–13, 7022 Leipzig. Tel: (341) 56 47 153
Rosenheimerstrasse 116b, Haus 93 (Kustermann Park), D-8000
   Munich 80. Tel: (89) 401832
**Goethe Institute** – 50 Princes Gate, London SW7 2PH. Tel: (020) 7581
   3344. Email: goethe.lon@dial.pipex.com
   Web site: *www.goethe.de/gr/lon/enindex.htm*
**MELTA (Munich English Language Teachers Association)** – Cramer
   Klett Str 2, 85579 Neubiberg
**ELTA Rhine** – Erich Muller Strasse 20, 40597 Dusseldorf
**International House** – IH Poststrasse 51, 20354 Hamburg
IH LGS Sprachkurse, Werderring 18, D-79098 Freiburg
**inLingua** – (amongst others) iL Aachen, Markt 29–31, D-52062
   Aachen
iL Braunschweig, Munzstrasse 15, D-38100 Braunschweig
iL Dresden, St Petersburger Str 26, D-01069 Dresden
**Berlitz** – Friedrich-Willhelm-Strasse 30, 47051 Duisburg
**Linguarama** – Linguarama Sprachinstitut, Kant Strasse 150, 10623
   Berlin

### Other school contacts

- Anglo-German Institute, Christopher St 4, 70178 Stuttgart
- Christopher Hills School of English, Sandeldamm 12, 63450
   Hanau
- GLS sprachenzentrum, B Jaeshke, Pestalozzi Str 886, 10625
   Berlin
- Intercom Lang Services, Muggenkampstr 38, 20257 Hamburg
- Lingotek Institut, Schlueterstrasse 18, 20146 Hamburg
- Yes Your English Services, Altonaer Chaussee 87, 22559
   Schenefeld, Hamburg

### GREECE

**Embassy** – 1a Holland Park, London W11 3TP. Tel: (020) 7229 3850
**British Council** – 17 Plateia Philikis Etairias, Kolonaki Square, PO
   Box 34388, Athens 10210. Tel: (1) 363 3211
Ethnikis Amynis 9/ Tsimiski Corner (PO Box 3488), 54013
   Thessalonika. Tel: (31) 23 52 36/7
**Ministry of Education** – 15 Mitropoleos Street, Athens
**TESOL Greece** – 87 Academis Street, Athens

## Other school contacts
- A Trechas Language Centre, 20 Koundouriotou St, Keratsini
- Eurocentre, 7 Solomou St, 41222 Larissa
- Kakkos School of English, Constantine Kakkos, A'Par. Papastratou 5, Arginio 30100
- Protypo English Language School, 22 Deliyioryi Street, Volos 3821
- Universal School of Language, 66 M Alexandrou Street, Panorama, Thessalonika 55200
- English Tuition Centre, 3 Pythias Street, Kypseli 1136, Athens

## HONG KONG

**Hong Kong Government Office** – 6 Grafton Street, London W1X 3LB. Tel: (020) 7499 9821
**British Council** – 3 Supreme Court Road, Admiralty, Hong Kong
**Directorate of Education** – Lee Gardens 5f, 33–37 Hysan Avenue, Causeway Bay, HK
**Hong Kong University Press** – 139 Pokfulam Road.
**Berlitz** – 1 Pacific Place, Central

## Other school contacts
- The Centre for Professional and Business English, 7th Floor, Core B, Hong Kong Polytechnic University, TST
- Hong Kong Association for Applied Linguistics, English Dept, Lingnan College, Fu Tei, Tuen Mun, New Territories
- Open University of Hong Kong, 30 Good Shepherd Street, Ho Man Tin, Kowloon
- City University of Hong Kong, Personnel Office, 4/F Cheng Yick-Shi Building, 83 Tat Chee Ave, Kowloon
- Hong Kong Baptist University, Language Centre, 224 Waterloo Road, Kowloon
- Pasona Education, 2/F One Hysan Ave, Causeway Bay

## HUNGARY

**Embassy** – 35 Eaton Place, London SW1X 8BY. Tel: (020) 7235 2664
**British Council** – Benczúr Utca 26, H-1068 Budapest. Tel: (1) 121 4039/1420918
**Ministry of Education** – Szalayu U 10/14, 1055 Budapest
**English Teachers Association of Hungary** – Dozsa Gyorgy ut 104.II, 15 068 Budapest

**International House** – IH Budapest, Bimbo ut 7, 1022 Budapest
IH 330 Eger, Mecset u.3

## Other school contacts

- Avalon '92 Agency, Erzsebet Krt 15, 1/19, 1073 Budapest
- Business Polytechnic, 1096 Vendel u.3/b, Budapest
- Karinthy Frigyes Gimnazium, Thokoly Utca 7, Pestlorinc, 1183 Budapest
- Western Maryland College Budapest, 1114 Villanyi ut 11–13, Budapest
- Budenz Jozsef High School Foundation, 1021 Budenz ut 20–22, Budapest
- International Business School, 1115 Etele u.68, Budapest

## INDONESIA

**Embassy** – 38 Grosvenor Square, London W1X 9AD. Tel: (020) 7499 7661
**British Council** – S Widjojo Centre, 71 Jalan Jenderal Sudirman, Jakarta 12190. Tel: (21) 522 3250
**Ministry of Education** – Jalan Jenderal Sudirman, Senayan, Jakarta Pusat
**inLingua** – Sekolah BHK, Jl Rahayu No 22, Daan Mogot, Jakarta Barat 11460
**EF English First** – Wisma Tamara Lt 4, Suite 402, Jl Jend Surdiman Kav 24, Jakarta 12920
EF Plaza Surabaya, Jl Pemuda 33–37, Surabaya 60271

## Other school contacts

- The British Institute (TBI), Plaza Setiabudi 2, Jalan HR Rasuna Said, Jakarta 12920
- International Language Programs (ILP), Jalan Raya Pasar Minguu No. 39A, Jakarta 12780
- School for International Training (SIT), Jalan Sunda 3, Menteng, Jakarta Pusat 10350
- Centre for Language Training (CLT), Soegijapranata Catholic University, Jl, Menteri Supeno 35, Semarang 50241
- International Language Studies (ILS), Jalan Ngemplak 30, Arbengan Plaza B-34, Surabaya 60272
- Strive International, Setiabudi 1 Building, Jalan HR Rasuna Said, Jakarta 12920

## IRELAND

**ATT (Association for Teacher Training in TEFL)** – PO Box 3384, Dublin 6

**NATEFL (National Association of Teachers of EFL in Ireland)** – PO Box 1917, Dublin 6

**RESLA (Recognised English Language Schools Association)** – 17 Camden St Lower, Dublin 2

### Other school contacts

- The Academy of English Studies, 33 Dawson St, Dublin 2
- Barkley Language School, 366 Sundays Well, Naas, Co Kildare
- Centre of English Studies, 31 Dame Street, Dublin 2
- Donegal Language School, Clemenstown, Ballylar, Letterkenny, Co Donegal
- Dublin Summer School, PO Box 2659, Dublin 6
- English Language Institute, 99 St Stephens Green, Dublin 2. Email: elin@iol.ie Web site: *www.englishlanguage.com*

## ITALY

**Embassy** – 14 Three Kings Yard, London W1Y 2EH. Tel: (020) 7629 8200

**Consulate** – 38 Eaton Place, London W1

111 Piccadilly, Manchester 2

7–9 Greyfriars, Bedford MK40 1HJ

**British Council** – Palazzo del Drago, Via Quatro Fontane 20, 00184 Rome. Tel: (6) 482 6641/8

Casa Isolani, Strada Maggiore 19, 40125 Bologna. Tel: (51) 225142

Via Manzoni 38, 20121 Milan. Tel: (2) 78 20 16-8

Palazzo d'Avalos, Via dei Mille 48, 80121 Naples. Tel: (81) 414876

**Italian Institute** – 39 Belgrave Square, London SW1X 8NX.

**Ministry of Education** – Viale Trastavere 76A, 00100 Rome

**International House** (amongst others) IH Via Zurlo 5, 86100 Compobasso

IH La Spezia, Via Manzoni 64, 19100 La Spezia

IH Roma, Viale Manzoni 22, 00185 Roma.
Email: ihroma.mz@ihromamz.it Web site: *www.ihromamz.it*

**inLingua** – (amongst others) iL Albano Laziale, Matteotti 178, I-0041 Albano Laziale

iL Bologna, Via Testoni 2, I-40123 Bologna

iL Foggia, Via Bari 72, I-71100 Foggia

**Berlitz** – Via delle Asole 2, Milano

## Other school contacts

- Academia Britannica, Via Bruxelles 61, 04100 Latina
- Bari Poggiofranco English Centre, Viale Pio XII 18, 70124 Bari
- British Institute of Florence, Palazzo Feroni, Via Tornalbuoni 2, Florence
- The British School, Via C Rasalba 49, Bari
- Cambridge Centre of English, Via Campanella 16, 41100 Modena
- Centro Lingue Moderne – The Bell Educational Trust, Via Canella 14, 38066 Riva del Garda

## JAPAN

**Embassy** – 101–104 Piccadilly, London W1V 9FN. Tel: (020) 7465 6500

**British Council** – c/o Cambridge English School, 2 Kaguruzaka 1-Chome, Shinjuku-ku, Tokyo 162. Tel: (3) 3235 8031

77 Kitashirakawa, Nishi-Machi, Sakyo-ku, Kyoto 606. Tel: (75) 791 7151

**Ministry of Education** – 3–2 Kasumigaseki, Chiyoda-ku, Tokyo

**AJET (Association for Japan Exchange and Teaching)** – AJET Drop Box, 4F Nissaykojimachi Building, 3–3–6 Kudan Machi, Chiyoda-ku, Tokyo 102

**JALT (The Japan Association of Language Teachers)** – Central Office, Urban Edge Bldg, 5th Floor, 1–37–9 Taito, Taito-ku, Tokyo 110

**inLingua** – iL Tokyo, 9F Kyodo Bldg, 2–4–2 Nihonbashi-Muromachi, Chuo-ku, Tokyo 103

**Berlitz** – Head Office, Kowa Bldg, 1,5f, 11–41, Alaska 1-chome, Minato-ku, Tokyo 107

## Other school contacts

- Aeon Institute of Foreign Languages, 7f Nihonseimei Building, 1–1, 3 Shimoishii, Okayama-shi 700
- CA English Academy, 2nd Floor, Kotohira Building, 9–14 Kakuozandori, Chikusa-ku, Nagoya
- EEC Foreign Languages Institute, Shikata Building 2f, 4–43 Nakazald-Nishi 2-chome, Kita-ku, Osaka 530
- Gateway Gakuin Rokko, Atelier House, 3–1–15 Yamada-cho, Nada-ku, Kobe

- Kains English School in Gakko, 1–5–2 Ohtemon Chuo-ku, Fukuoka 810
- MIL Language Centre, 3.4F Eguchi Bldg, 1–6–2 Katsutadai, Yachiyo-shi, Chiba-ken 276

## KOREA (SOUTH)

**Embassy** – 60 Buckingham Gate, London SW1E. Tel: (020) 7227 5500

**British Council** – Room 401, Anglican Church Annex, 3–7 Chung Dong, Choong-ku, Seoul 100–120. Tel: (2) 737 7157

**Ministry of Education** – 77–6 Sejong-no, Chongno-ku, Seoul

**Korea TESOL** – Joo-kung Park, Dept of English, Honam University, 59–1 Seobong-dong, Kwangszan-gu, Kwanglu 506–090

**inLingua** – iL Seoul, 5-6F Mikwan Building, 63 Suhadong, Chunggu, 100–210 Seoul

**Berlitz** – Sungwood Academy Building 2F, 1316–17 Seocho-Dong, Seocho-Gu, Seoul 137–074. Email: mpbubb@yahoo.com

### Other school contacts
- Best Foreign Language Institute, 98–3 Jungang-Dong, Chang-won City, Kyungsangnam Province 641-030
- Keimyung Junior College, 2139 Dae-Myung Dong, Nam-ku, Taegu 705-037
- Pagoda Language School, 56–6 2nd Street, Jong-ro, Seoul 110-122
- Chuncheon National University of Education, Chuncheon 200-703
- Korea Foreign Language Institute, 16–1 Kwancheol-Dong, Chongro-ku, Seoul
- Prime English Language School, 240 Doryang Dong, Kumi, Kyunguk Province

## LATVIA

**Embassy** – 45 Nottingham Place, London W1M 3FE. Tel: (020) 7312 0040

**British Council** – Blaumana Iela 5a, Riga 1011

**Ministry of Education** – Valnu Iela 2, Riga 1098

## Other school contacts

- English Language Centre 'Satva', Office 8, 79/85 Dzirnavu Str, Riga LV-1011
- International Centre 'R&V' 10, Meistaru Str, Riga, LV-1050
- Jurmala Language Centre, 4 Ogres Str, Jurmala, LV-2000-04-20
- Language centre 'Meridian', 9-210 Juras str, Ventaplla, LV-3600
- Public Service Language Unit, 3/1 Smilieu Str, Riga, LV-1838
- 'Mirte', 23 Raina Bulv, Riga, LV-1050

## LITHUANIA

**Embassy** – 84 Gloucester Place, London W1H. Tel: (020) 7486 6401
**British Council** – Teachers Resource Centre, Vilnaius 39/6, Vilnius 2001.
**Ministry of Education** – A Volano 2/7, Vilnius 2691
**International House** – Soros IH, Gedimino 47, 3000 Kaunas
Soros IH, Ukmerges 41, 2662 Vilnius
**EF English First** – Kosciuskos g.11, 2000 Vilnius

## Other school contacts

- Klaipeda International School of Languages, Zuejug, 25 800, Klaipeda
- Siauliai Pedagogical Institute, P. Visinskio 25, 5419 Siauliai
- English Language Teaching Centre, Rinktines 28a, Vilnius 2051
- Poliglotas, Foreign Language Courses, Ozo 17–12, Vilnius
- Foreign Language Courses, Kauno 1a, Vilnius
- A.Sakalienes Foreign Language School, See and Learn, Zirmunu 37, Vilnius 2012

## MACEDONIA

**Embassy** – Suite 10, Harcourt House, 19A Cavendish Square, London W1M 9AD. Tel: (020) 7499 5152
**British Council** – British Information Centre, Bulevar Goce Delcev 6, PO Box 562, 91000 Skopje.
**Ministry of Education** – 9 Ulica Veljko Vlahovic, 91000 Skopje
**International House** – Soros IH, Nikola Parapunov bb, 91000 Skopje

## Other school contacts

- Letikom Plus, Bojmija 8, 91000 Skopje

- Lili School of English, Ul. AFZ 7b, 91000 Skopje
- Lingual, Ograzden 1–1/2, 91000 Skopje
- London-City, Aco Karamanov 13, 91000 Skopje
- Pro-Lingua, Bul. Jane Sandanski 36/II/22, 91000 Skopje
- Queen, Ul. Naroden Front 5/II/5, 91000 Skopje

## MALAYSIA

**High Commission** – 45-46 Belgrave Square, London SW1X 8QT. Tel: (020) 7235 8033

**British Council** – Jalan Bukit Aman, PO Box 10539, 50480 Kuala Lumpur. Tel: (3) 298 7555/230 6304

Wisma Esplanade, 43 Green Hall, PO Box 595, 10770 Penang. Tel: (4) 630330

Unit 14.01, Level 14, Wisma LKN, 49 Jalan Wong Ah Fook, PO Box 8, 80700 Johor Bahru. Tel: (7) 233340

**Ministry of Education** – Block J, Pusat Level 9, Bandar Damansara, 50604 Kuala Lumpur

### Other school contacts

- Advanced Management College, 2nd Floor, Block A Karamunsing Complex, 88000 Kota Kinabalu, Sabah
- Kinabalu College, 3rd Floor Wisma Sabah, 88000 Kota Kinabalu, Sabah
- Tunka Putra International School, Jalan Nanas, 93400 Kuching, Sarawak
- Inti College, Jalan Stampin Timur, 93350 Kuching, Sarawak
- Stamford College, Bangunan Binamas, Jalan Padungan, 93100 Kuching, Sarawak
- International English Centre, Kompleks Sunny, Mile 11/2 Tuaran Road, 88100 Kota Kinabalu, Sabah

## MALTA

**High Commission** – 36–38 Piccadilly, London W1V. Tel: (020) 7292 4800

**British Council** – 89 Archbishop Street, Valletta, VLT 12. Tel: 224707

**Ministry of Education** Floriana CMR 02

**inLingua** 9 Triq Guzè fava, Tower Road, Sliema SLM 15.

**Other school contacts**

- Students Travel School, c/o St Aloysius College, Bkara
- Elanguest, Keating House, Ross Street, St Julians
- International English Language Centre, 78 Tigne Street, Sliema SLM11
- Revival English Language Institute, Trinity Hall, Taliana Lane, Gzira
- Magister Academy, L-Arkati, Mensija St, St Julians
- Link School of English, Link Court, 27 Victoria Junction, Sliema

## MEXICO

**Embassy** – 43 Hertford Street, London W1Y 7TF. Tel: (020) 7459 8568

**Consulate** – 8 Halkin Street, London SW1X 7DW. Tel: (020) 7235 6393

**British Council** – Maestro Antonio Caso 127, Col San Rafael, Apdo Postal 30-588, Mexico 06470 DF. Tel: (5) 566 6144

**Ministry of Education** – República de Argentina y Gonzales Obregón 28, 06029 Mexico DF

**EF English First** – Londres 188, Col Juarez, CP 06600, Mexico DF

**Other school contacts**

- Anglo-Mexican Cultural Institute, Rio Nazas 116, Colonia Cuauhtémoc, 06500 Mexico DF
- Instituto Franklin de Yucatan, Calle 57, No 474-A, 9700 Merida, Yucatan
- Universidad Autonoma de Baja California Sur, Carr. Al Sur, Km 5.5, 23080 La Paz, Bcs.
- Universidad de Guadalajara, Escuela Superior de Lenguas Modernas, Apdo.Postal 2–416, 44280 Guadalajara, Jal.
- Universidad Autonoma de San Luis Potosi, Centro de Idiomas, Zaragoza No 410, 78200 San Luis Potosi, SLP.
- Colegio Internacional de Cuernavaca, Apartado Postal 1334, Cuernavaca, Morelos

## MOROCCO

**Embassy** – 49 Queens Gate, London SW7 5NE. Tel: (020) 7581 5001

**British Council** – 36 rue de Tanger, BP 427, Rabat. Tel: (7) 760836

**Ministry of Education** – Quartier des Ministères, Rabat

**EF English First** – 20 rue du Marche, Residence Benomar, Maaris, Casablanca.

## Other school contacts

- Bénedict School of English, 124 Ave Hassan II, Ben Slimane
- London School of English, 10 ave des FAR, Casablanca
- British Centre, 3 rue Nolly, Casablanca
- British and Professional English Centre (BPEC), 74 rue Jean Jaures, Casablanca
- Institut Cegis, 23 Boulevard Ibnou Makid Al Bahhar, Casablanca
- International Language Centre, 2 rue Tihama, Rabat

## NETHERLANDS

**Embassy** – 38 Hyde Park Gate, London SW7 5DP. Tel: (020) 7590 3200

**British Council** – MD Keizersgracht 343, 1016 EH Amsterdam. Tel: (20) 622 36 44

**Ministry of Education** – Post Bus 25000, 2700 LZ Zoetermeer

**CITO-TOEFL** – PO Box 1203, 6801 BE Arnhem

**Berlitz** – Rokin 87-89, 1012 Kl Amsterdam

**Linguarama** – Wtc Strawinskylaan 507, 1077 Amsterdam
Venestraat 27, 2525 Ca Den Haag

## Other school contacts

- Amerongen Talenpraktikum, De Kievit 1, 3958 Dd Amerongen
- Boerhave Opleidingen, Hoogsrtaat 118, 801 Bb Zwolle
- Eerste Nederlandse Talenpraktikum, Kalverstr 112, 1012 Pk Amsterdam
- Instituut Meppel, Tav Dhr J G Rijpkema, Postbus 263, 7940 Ag Meppel
- Language Partners Rotterdam, Wtc Beursplein 37, 3011 A Rotterdam
- Onderwijsinstituut Netty Post, Haverstraat 2, 1447 Ce Purmerend

## NEW ZEALAND

**High Commission** – New Zealand House, Haymarket, London SW1Y 4TQ. Tel: (020) 7930 8422

**British Council** – c/o British High Commission, 44 Hill Street, PO Box 1812, Wellington 1

**Department of Education** – Private Bag, Wellington. Web site: *www.teachnz.govt.nz*

**FIELS (Federation of Independent English Language Schools)** – PO Box 2577, Auckland

**NZEIL (New Zealand Education International Ltd)** – PO Box 10500, Wellington

## Other school contacts

- ABC College of English, PO Box 755, Queenstown
- Auckland English Academy, PO Box 11241, Ellerslie, Auckland
- Central Institute of Technology, Private Bag, Wellington Mail Centre, Wellington
- Dominion English School (Christ.), PO Box 3908, Christchurch
- ILA South Pacific Ltd, PO Box 25170, Christchurch 1
- Language Institute, University of Waikato, Private Bag 3105, Hamilton

## NORWAY

**Embassy** – 25 Belgrave Square, London SW1X 8QD. Tel: (020) 7235 7151

**British Council** – Fridtjof Nansens Plass 5, 0160 Oslo 1. Tel: 22 42 68 48

**Ministry of Education** – PO Box 8119, 0032 Oslo

**LMS (Modern Languages Association of Norway)** – Jonas Liesvei, 1B 1412 Sofiemyr

**Berlitz** – Lille Grensen 5, 0159 Oslo

## Other school contacts

- Folkeuniversitetet/Friundervisningen Oslo, Torggata 7 (PB 496 Sentrum), 0105 Oslo. Email: info@fu.oslo.no
- Atlas Sprakreiser, Postboks 191, Vindern, 0319 Oslo
- Noricom Spraktjenester, Batstadstien 4, 4056 Tananger
- Allegro A/S Spraktjenester, Strandkaien 6, 5013 Bergen
- English Language Centre, Lokkev.16, 4008 Stavanger
- Norsk Sprakinstitut, Kongensgt.9, 0153 Oslo. Email: snorsk@online.no

## PERU

**Embassy** – 52 Sloane Street, London SW1X 9SP. Tel: (020) 7235 6867

**British Council** – Calle Alberto Lynch 110, San Isidro, Lima 14. Tel: (14) 70 43 50

**Ministry of Education** – Parque Universitario s/n, Lima

**inLingua** – iL Lima, Av. L M Sanchez Cerro 2144–2150, Jesus Maria, Lima 11

### Other school contacts

- Associación Cultural Peruano Britanico, Av.Arequipa 3495, San Isidro, Lima
- Interaction in English, Manco Capac 649, Miraflores, Lima 18
- CENE Cambridge, Los Abanicos 222, La Encantada de Villa, Chorrillos, Lima 9
- Markham College Lower School, Avda. El Derby, Cdra 3/Esq. Avda El Carmen, Surco
- Colegio Newton, Av. Elias Aparicio s/n, La Molina, Lima 12
- Markham College Upper School, Augusto Angulo 291, San Antonio, Miraflores, Lima 18

## POLAND

**Embassy** – 47 Portland Place, London W1N 3AG. Tel: (020) 7580 4324

**British Council** – Al Jerozolimskie 59, 00-697 Warsaw. Tel: (2) 628 74 01/3

**Cultural Institute** – 34 Portland Place, London W1N 4HQ. Tel: (020) 7636 6032

**Ministry of Education** – Al J Ch Szucha 25, 00-918 Warsaw.

**FIPLV** – Adam Micklewickz University, 28 Czerwca 1956 nr 198, PL-61-485 Poznan

**Soros Foundation** – Batory Foundation, – 9 Flory St, 4th Floor, 00-586 Warsaw

**International House** – (amongst others) IH Wroclaw, ul Ruska 46a, 50 079 Wroclaw. Email: jonbutt@silesia.top.pl Web site: *www.silesia.top.pl/~ihih/katowice.*

IH ul Zielona 15, 90-601 Lodz

IH ul Gliwicka 10, 40-079 Katowice

**inLingua** – ul Morska 55, PL-10-145 Olsztyn

**Berlitz** – ul Wiejska 12a, Warszawa 00 490

Jupiter Centrum, ul Miedzianall, Warszawa 00 835
ul Nowogrodzka 56, Warszawa 00 695
**EF English First** – Smolna 8, P18, 00375 Warszawa
**Linguarama** – Linguarama Polska, SP Z.O.O., ul Sniadeckich 17,
Warszawa 00 654. Email: Linguarama_War@compuserve.com
Web site: *www.linguarama.com*

### Other school contacts
- ABC Szkola Jezkow Obcych, ul Wiktorska 30, Warszawa 02 587
- Anglomer, ul Panska 5/18, Warszawa 00 124
- Brams, ul Koncertowa 8, Warszawa 02 784
- Cambridge School of English, ul Wiertnicza 26, Warszawa 02 952
- Eibisi, ul Dantego 7/243, Warszawa 01 914
- English Language Studio, ul Jadzwingow 1 m 34, Warszawa 02
  692


## PORTUGAL

**Embassy** – 11 Belgrave Square, London SW1X 8PP. Tel: (020) 7235
5331
**Consulate** – 62 Brompton Road, London SW3 1BJ. Tel: (020) 7581
8722
**British Council** – Rua de São Marcal 174, 1294 Lisbon Codex. Tel:
347 6141
Casa da Inglaterra, Rua de Tomar 4, 3000 Coimbra. Tel: 23549
Rua do Breiner 155, 4000 Porto. Tel: 200 5577
Rua Dr.Camilo Dionisio Alvares, Lote 6, 2775 Parede, Cascais. Tel:
457 3414
**Ministry of Education** – Avenida 5 de Outubro 107, 1000 Lisbon
**APPI (Associação Portuguesa de Profesores de Inglês)** – Apartado
2885, 1122 Lisbon
**International House** (amongst others), IH Rua Domingos Carran-
cho 1-1- Dt, 3800 Aveiro
IH Rua Miguel Bombarda 3–1, 2560 Torres Vedras
IH Lisbon, Rua Marques Sá de Bandeira 16, 1000 Lisboa
**inLingua** iL Lisboa, Rua Rodrigo da Fonseca 60–2 Dto, P–1250
Lisboa
iL Porto, Rua Gonçalo Cristovão 217–12, P–4000 Porto
iL Campo Grande 30–1A, 1700 Lisboa
**Berlitz** – Av.Conde Valbom 6–4, 1000 Lisboa

## Other school contacts

- Big Ben School, Rua Moinho Fanares 4–1, 2725 Mem Martins
- Centro de Estudos IPFEL, Rua Edith Cavell 8, 1900 Lisboa
- Centro de Linguas de Queluz, Av. Dr Miguel Bombarda 62–l'Esq, 2745 Queluz
- Ecubal-Lombos, Barros Brancos, Porches, 8400 Lagoa
- English School of Loulé, Rua José F Guerreiro 66M, Galerias do Mercado, 8100 Loulé
- IF Inglês Funcional, Rua Afonso Alburquerque 73-a, 2460 Alcobaça

## ROMANIA

**Embassy** – 4 Palace Green, London W8 4QD. Tel: (020) 7937 9666
**British Council** – Calea Dorobalintor 14, Bucharest. Tel: (1) 312 0314
**Ministry of Education** – Str. Gen.Berthelot 28–30, 70663 Bucharest
**International House** – IH Timisoara, Bl. Republicii 9, 1900 Timisoara. Email: rodica@ihlctim.sorostm.ro

## Other school contacts

- ACCESS Language Centre, Str Tebei nr 21, 3400 CLUJ–Napoca
- CLASS (Constanta Language Assoc.), Str Mircea cel Batran nr 103, 8700 Constanta
- International Language Centre, Str Moara de Foc nr 35, Et 8, 6600 Iasi
- PROSPER – ASE Language Centre, Suite 4211, et 2, Calea Griveti 2–2A, Bucharest
- PROSPER – Transilvania Language Centre, Str Carpilator 15/17 (ICIM), 2200 Brasov
- RALEX Linguistic Centre, Str Buna Vestire nr 35, 1000 Ramnicu Valeca

## RUSSIA

**Embassy** – 18 Kensington Palace Gardens, London W8 4QX. Tel: (020) 7229 6412
**British Council** – Biblioteka Inostrannoi Literaturi, Ulitsa nikolo-Yamskaya 1, Moscow 109189 Tel: (095) 297 3499
**Ministry of Education** – Christoprudny Bul 6, Moscow
**NLELTA** – 31a Minin St, Nizhny Novgorod 603155

**SPELTA** – No 31 Ordzonikiolze Str, Corp 1, Flat 133, Saint Petersburg 196158

**International House** – BKC IH, Vsevolozhsky per d 2, Moscow 1 19034. Email: bkc.ih@g23.relcom.ru Web site: *www.bkc.ru*

BKC IH, Building 4, 9a Tverskaya St, Moscow 103009

BKC IH, Dom 8A, YBK 1806 Rodnik, Berezovaya Alleya, Zelenograd, 103498 Moscow

**EF English First** – 125 Brestkaya 1st Street, 5th Floor, 125047 Moscow.

**Linguarama** – 2nd Floor, Rm 62, Maly Ziatoustonsky per 6, Moscow 101863

### Other school contacts

- Benedict School, Chapliginia 92, Novosibirsk 630099
- Centre for Intensive Foreign Language Instruction, Sparrow Hills, Building 2, Moscow 119899
- Link School of Languages, 15/81 pl Lenina, 394000 Voronezh
- Polyglot ILA, Block 5, 19 Novoyasenevsky Prospekt, Moscow 117593. Email: polyglot@glasnet.ru
- System-3 Language & Communication, Kantemirovskaya Street 16 #531, Moscow 115522
- Breitner Language School, Leninsky Prospekt 29, Britner Ltd, Tatyana, Karmanova

### SAUDI ARABIA

**Royal Embassy** – 30 Charles Street, London W1X 7PM. Tel: (020) 7917 3000

**British Council** – Olaya Main Road, Al Mousa Centre, Tower B, 3rd Floor, Office 235, PO Box 58012, Riyadh 11594. Tel: (1) 462 1818/464 4928

4th Floor, Middle East Centre, Falasteen St (PO Box 3424), Jeddah 21471. Tel: ( 2) 672 3336

Al-Mowajil Building, Dhahran St/ Mohammed St, PO Box 8387, Dammam 31482. Tel: (3) 834 3484

**Ministry of Education** – PO Box 3734, Airport Road, Riyadh

**Education Office** – 29 Belgrave Square, London SW1X 9QB. Tel: (020) 7245 6481

**British Aerospace** – Saudi Arabia Support Dept, Warton Aerodrome, Preston, Lancs. PR4 1LA. Tel: (01772) 634317. Fax: (01772) 852096

## Other school contacts

- Girls College of Arts – General Presidency for Female Institute for Languages and Translation, c/o King Saud University, PO Box 2465, Riyadh 11451
- King Fahd University of Petroleum & Minerals English Language Centre, Dhahran 31261
- Riyadh Military Hospital, Training Division, PO Box 7897, Riyadh 11159
- Saudi Airlines, PO Box 167, Jeddah 21231
- Saudi Language Institute, PO Box 6760, Riyadh 11575
- SCECO East Central Training Institute, PO Box 5190, Damman 31422

## SINGAPORE

**High Commission** – 9 Wilton Crescent, London SW1X 8SA. Tel: (020) 7235 8315

**British Council** – 30 Napier Road, Singapore 1025. Tel: 473 1111

**Ministry of Education** – Kay Siang Road, Singapore 1024

**International House** – IH Singapore/ATT, Tanglin Shopping Centre, 19 Tanglin Road, Singapore 247909

**inLingua** – 68 Orchard Rd, 07–04 Plaza Singapura, Singapore 238839

1 Graneg Road, 04–01, Orchard Building, Singapore 239683

**Berlitz** – 501 Orchard Road, B1–20, Orchard MRT Station, Singapore 238878

**Linguarama** – 220 Orchard Rd 02–09, Midpoint Orchard Sports, Singapore 238852

## Other school contacts

- Coleman Commercial and Language Centre, Peninsula Plaza, Singapore
- International School, 21 Preston Rd, Singapore 0410
- Lorna Whiston Study Centre (primary), 583 Orchard Rd, 05–04 Forum Galeria, Singapore 238884
- Stamford City School of Commerce, 192 Waterloo Street, 5th Floor Skyline Building, Singapore 0718
- Corrine Private School, Selegie Complex 04–227, Selegie Rd, Singapore 188350
- Julia Gabriel Communications, 13 Halifax Road, Singapore

## SLOVAK REPUBLIC ( SLOVAKIA)

**Embassy** – 25 Kensington Palace Gardens, London W8 4QY. Tel: (020) 7243 0803
**British Council** – PO Box 68, Panská 17, 81101 Bratislava. Tel: (7) 331074
**Ministry of Education** – Hlboka 2, 813 30 Bratislava
**Berlitz** Jazykova Skola, Na Vrska 2, 811 01 Bratislava

### Other school contacts
- Akademia Vzdelavania, Druzstevna 2, 831 03 Bratislava
- Effective Language Centre, Biela 3, 040 01 Kosice
- Eurolingua, Jazykova Skola sro, Drienova 16, 821 03 Bratislava
- Jazykova Skola EURO, Nabrezna 30, 940 75 Nove Zamky
- Lingua Jazykova Skola, Zahradnick 2, 931 01 Samorin
- Pro Sympatia, Centrum Studia Cudzich Jazykov, Pribinova 23, 810 11 Bratislava

## SLOVENIA

**Embassy** – Suite 1, Cavendish Court, 11–15 Wigmore Street, London W1H 9LA. Tel: (020) 7495 7775
**British Council** – Stefanova 1/III, 61000 Ljubljana
**Ministry of Education** – Zupanciceva 6, 61000 Ljubljana

### Other school contacts
- Accent on Language d.o.o., Ljubljanska c.36, 1230 Domzale
- Cenca p.o., Masarykova c. 18/Ribnisko selo, 2000 Maribor Dialog d.o.o.
- Flamingo d.o.o., Pod Gonjami 44, 2391 Prevalje
- Jezikovni Biro Lindic, Cankarjeva ul 10, 2000 Maribor
- Ljudiska Univerza Nova Gorica, Cankarjeva ul 8, 5000 Noca Gorica
- Multilinga d.o.o., Ulica Bratov Hvalic 16, 5000 Nova Gorica

## SOUTH AFRICA

**High Commission** – South Africa House, Trafalgar Square, London WC2N 5DP. Tel: (020) 7930 4488
**British Council** – 76 Juta Street, PO Box 30637, Braamfontein 2017.
**Dept of National Education** – Private Bag X603, Shoeman Street, Magister Building, Pretoria 0001

**Education and Culture Service** – Private Bag 9008, Cape Town 8000

**International House** – IH Cape Town, Windermere, Portswood Business Park, V & A Waterfront, Cape Town 8002, PO Box 52199

**inLingua** – 27 Dixon Street, Cape Town 8001

### Other school contacts

- Academic Support Programme, PO Wits, Johannesburg 2050
- English Language Educational Trust, 6th Floor, Wesley Building, 74 Aliwal Street, Durban 4000
- Language Wise, Cargo House, Car jan, Smuts & 7th St, Rosebank, Johannesburg
- Cape Town TEFL School of English and Foreign Languages, Manya Brodell, Morkels Building, 66 Main Road, Claremont 7700, Cape Town
- Interman, PO Box 52621, Saxonworld, Johannesburg 2132
- Studywell College, 102 De Korte Street, Braamfontein, Johannesburg 2000

## SPAIN

**Embassy** – 39 Chesham Place, London SW1X 8QA. Tel: (020) 7235 5555

**Consulate** – 20 Draycott Place, London SW3

21 Rodnet Road, Liverpool L1 9EF

70 Spring Gardens, Manchester M2 2BQ

**British Council** – Calle Almagro 5, 28010 Madrid. Tel: (1) 337 3500

British Institute, Residencia Universitaria Esteban Terradas, Plaza de la Casilla 3, 48012 Bilbao. Tel: (0) 444 6666

Calle Amigo 83, 08021 Barcelona. Tel: (3) 209 1364

Edificio Atalaya, Calle Azhuma 5, 18003 Granada. Tel: (58) 267913

British Institue, Bravo Murillo 25, 35003 Las Palmas de Gran Canaria. Tel: (28) 36 83 00

Brit. Inst., Calle del Rosal 7, 33009 Oviedo. Tel: (85) 522 9430

Brit. Inst., Goethe 1, 07011 Palma de Mallorca. Tel: (71) 454855

Instituto Britanico en Segovia, Trinidad 3, 40001 Segovia. Tel: (11) 434813

c/o Brit. Consulate, Plaza Nueva 8b, 41001 Seville. Tel: (5) 422 8873

General San Martin 7, 46004 Valencia. Tel: (6) 352 9874

**Spanish Institute** – 102 Eaton Square, London SW1. Tel: 020-7235-1485

**Ministry of Education** – Alcal 34, 28071 Madrid
**APAC (Associaco de Professors d'Angles de Catalunya)** – Apartado 2287, 08080 Barcelona
**International House** – (amongst others) IH Trafalgar 14 Entlo, 08010 Barcelona. Email: training@bcn.ihes.com
Website: *www./ihes.com.bcn.*
IH Carrer Balmes 29, 08301 Mataro
IH Avinguda Diagonal 612 Entlo, 08021 Barcelona
**inLingua** – (amongst others) iL Albacete, Tesifonte Gallego 20, Apdo 14, E-02002 Albacete
iL Burgos, Perlado, Avda Eliado Perlado 31-1, E-09005 Burgos
iL Lleida, Alcalde Rovira Roure 9, E-25006 Lleida
**Berlitz** – Gran Via 80, 4, 28013, Madrid
Edif.Forum 1 Mod, 3 Av Luis Morales, S/N 41018 Sevilla
**Linguarama** – Gran Via de Carlos III 98- 2, Edificios Trade, 08028 Barcelona

### Other school contacts

- Academia Andaluza de Idiomas, Crta El Punto 9, Conil, Cadiz
- Afoban, Alfonso XII 30, 41002 Sevilla
- Ard Escuela de Idiomas, Alejandro del Castillo, 35100 Playa del Inglés, Gran Canaria
- Big Ben College, Plaza Quintiliano 13, Calahorra 26500 La Rioja
- British Language Centre, C/Bravo Murillo 377, 28020 Madrid
- Cambridge School, Plaça Manel Montanya 4, 08400 Granollers

### SWEDEN

**Embassy** – 11 Montagu Place, London W1H 2AL. Tel: (020) 7917 6400
**British Council** Skarpögarton 6, Box 27819, 11527 Stockholm. Tel: (8) 667 0140
**Ministry of Education** – Mynttorget 1, 103 33 Stockholm

### Other school contacts

- British Institute, Hagatan 3, 511348 Stockholm, Email: info@britishinstitute.se
- Folkuniversitetet, Box 26152, 100 41 Stockholm
- Language for Business, Ekbackev. 16, 181 46 Lidingo, Stockholm

- Internationella Skolorna, Box 26210, 100 41 Stockholm
- ALL-International Language Center AB, Morbydalen 25, Danderyd
- Pro Linguis, Hammarby Fabriksv. 21A, Box 17039, 104 62 Stockholm

## SWITZERLAND

**Embassy** – 16–18 Montagu Place, London W1H 2BQ. Tel: (020)7723-0701
**British Council** – British Embassy, Sennweg, Berne 9
**ETAS (English Teachers Association Switzerland)** – Gurzeingasse 25, 4500 Solothurn
**International House** – IH, St Gallen, Lindenstrasse 139, 9016 St Gallen
IH Regensford/ZH, Althardstrasse 70, 8105 Regensford
ASC IH , 72 rue de Lausanne, 1202 Geneva
**inLingua** – (amongst others) iL Basel, Heuberg 12, 2 Stock, CH-4051 Basel
iL Neuchatel, 18 Av de la Gare, CH-2000 Neuchatel
iL Fribourg, Rue St Pierre 4, CH-1700 Fribourg
**Berlitz** – 14 rue De L'Ancien-Port, 1202 Geneva
Munzgasse 3, 4001 Basel

### Other school contacts
- Basilingua Sprachschule, Birsigstrasse 2, 4054 Basel
- Institute Le Rosey, Camp d'Eté, Route des Quatre Communes, CH-1180 Rolle
- Bell Language School, 12 Chemin des Colombettes, 1202 Geneva
- Markus Frei Sprachenschule, Neugasse 6, 6300 Zug
- Village Camps, 1296 Coppet
- Volkschohschule, Splugenstrasse 10, Zurich 8002

## TAIWAN

**Taipei Rep Office in UK** – 50 Grosvenor Gardens, London SW1. Tel: (020) 7396 9152
**British Council** – 7th Floor, Fu Key Building, 99 Jen Al Road, Section 2, Taïpei 10625
**Ministry of Education** – 5 Chungshan South Road, Taipei 100

**Other school contacts**
- Apex English Group, Kwan Chien Rd, #28, Taipei
- Disney English, Hoping East Rd, Sec 2, Lane 96, Taipei
- ELSI English, Nan Yang St, #13, 7F, Taipei
- Han Bang Language School, Chung Yuan Rd, #17, 2F, Taipei
- Hua Ya English, Fu Hsing North Rd, #1, 2F, Taipei
- Jyu Hwei English, Roosevlt Trd, Sec 3, #302, B1 Taipei

## THAILAND

**Royal Embassy** – 30 Queens Gate, London SW7 5JB. Tel: (020) 7589 2944

**British Council** – 428 Rama 1 Road, Siam Square, Phyathai Road, Bangkok 10330. Tel: (2) 252 6136

198 Bumrungraj Road, Chiang Mai 50000. Tel: (53) 242103

**Ministry of Education** – Rajdamnern Avenue, Bangkok

**Thai TESOL** – 204/77 Phasukasem 3, Phatanakarn Rd, Parawet, Bangkok 10250

**inLingua** – Head Office, 7th Floor, Central Chidlom Tower, 22 Ploenchit Rd, Pathumwan, Bangkok 10330.
Email: executrn@ksc5.th.com

iL Silom , 20$^{th}$ floor, Liberty Square Bldg, 287 Silom Rd, Bangrak, Bangkok 10500

iL Piklao, 5$^{th}$ Floor, Central Plaza, Piklao Office Bldg, 7/129 Baromrajchonnee Rd, Bangkok 10700

**Berlitz** – Silom Complex 22F, 191 Silom Rd, 10500 Bangkok

**Other school contacts**
- ELS International, 419/2 Rajavithee Road, Phyathai, Bangkok 10400
- English Language Schools, 26/3, 26/9 Chonpol Lane 15, Bangkok 10900
- LCC Language Institute, 8/64–67 Ratchadapisek-Larprao Rd, Bangkhaen, Bangkok 10900
- Training Creativity Development (TCD), 399/7 Soi Thongloh 21, Sukhumvit Soi 55, Bangkok 10110
- Bangkok Patana First School, 2/38 Soi Lasalle, Sukhumvit 105, Bangkok 10260
- Maejo University, Western Languages Section, Faculty of Agricultural Business, Chiang Mai 50290.
  Email: lalida@maejo.mju.ac.th

## TURKEY

**Embassy** – 43 Belgrave Square, London SW1X 8PA. Tel: (020) 7393 0202

**British Council** – c/o British Embassy, Kirklangic Sokak 9, Gazi Osman pasa, 06700 Ankara. Tel: (4) 428 3165-9

Istaklal Caddesi 251/253, Kat 2–6, Galatasaray (PK 436 Beyoglu 80060), Istanbul. Tel: (1) 252 74 74-8

1481 Sokak, no 9, Alsancak, Izmir. Tel: (51) 220459

**Ministry of Education** – Milli Egitim Bakanligi, Ankara

**METU DBE (Department of Basic English)** – Ankara 06531

### Other school contacts

- Active English, Ybrahim Gokcen Bulvari No 50/1, Manisa
- Cambridge English, Kazim Ozalp Sok. No 15, Kat 4, Saskinbakkal, Istanbul
- English Academy, 858 Sok. Tarancilar y Hani No 5 K4, Konak, Yzmir
- English Star, Pehit Fethibey Caddesi, y Hani No 79/7, Pasaport, Yzmir
- Istanbul-Turco British Association, Suleyman Nazif Sokak 68, Nisantasi, 80220 Istanbul
- London Languages International, Abide-I Hurriyet Caddesi, Kat 1, Mecidiyekoy, Istanbul

## UKRAINE

**Embassy** – 78 Kensington Park Road, London W11 2PL. Tel: (020) 7727 6312

**British Council** – Kiev Polytechnic Institute, Room 258, 37 Peremogy Ave, 20 2056 Kiev. Tel: (44) 11495

**Ministry of Education** – Peremohy pr 10, 252135 Kiev

**International House** – 1 Universitetska St, 290602 Lviv

IH Kharkiv, 7 Marshala Bazhanova St, 31002 Kharkiv

IH Kiev, 7 V Vasilevskoy St, PO Box 64121, Kiev 252 055

### Other school contacts

- Interlingua, Kiev State Foreign Language Training, Glavnaya Korpus Instituta Fyskultura, Fyzkulturnaya 1, Kiev 252040
- Language Link Ukraine, Recruitment Section, 21 Harrington Rd, South Kensington, London SW7 3EU

- Kiev Institute of Interpreters, Tryokhsviatitelska St 4, Kiev 252601
- International Business Communication Language School, 84 Bozhenko Str, Rm 221, Kiev 252022
- Monarch International Language Academy, Vorovskogo 8, Appt 1/2, Kiev 252 000. Email: office@Monarch.Kiev.UA.
- London School of English, Kiev Polytechnic University, Bldg 19, Room 530, Kiev

## UNITED ARAB EMIRATES (UAE)

**Embassy** – 30 Princes Gate, London SW7 1PT. Tel: (020) 7581 1281
**British Council** – Saadaqua Tower, Nr Emirate Sloga Hotel Tourist Club Area, PO Box 46523 Abu Dhabi. Tel: (2) 788400
Tariq bin Zaid Street, Nr Rashid Hospital, PO Box 1636, Dubai. Tel: (4) 370109
PO Box 1870, Al Ain. Tel: (3) 643838
**Ministry of Education** – PO Box 295, Abu Dhabi
**TESOL Arabia** – University of UAE, English Unit, PO Box 17172, Al Ain

### Other school contacts

- Abu Dhabi National Oil Co, PO Box 898, Abu Dhabi
- Dubai Cultural and Scientific Institute, PO Box 8751, Dubai
- Polyglot School, PO Box 1093, Dubai
- Dar Al Ilm School of Languages, PO Box 2550, Dubai
- International Language Institute, Language Specialists Institute, PO Box 3253, Sharjah
- Arabic Language Centre, Dubai World Trade Centre, PO Box 9292, Dubai

## URUGUAY

**Embassy** – 140 Brompton Road, London SW3 1HY. Tel: (020) 7589 8735
**Ministry of Education** – Sarandi 440, Montevideo
**British Embassy** – Calle Marco Bruto 1073, PO Box 16024, Montevideo 11300
**URUTESOL** – Colonia 1342, Piso 7, Montevideo 11100

## Other school contacts

- British Schools, Maximo Tajes esq Havre, Carrasco, Montevideo
- Dickens Institute, 21 de Setiembro, 3090, CP 11300 Montevideo
- English Studio Centre, Obligado 1221, Montevideo
- English Lighthouse Institute, Sarandi 881, Maldonado
- Instituto Cultural Anglo-Urugayo, Casilla de Correos 5087 Sec 1, San José 1426, Montevideo 11300
- London Institute School of Languages, Caramuru 5609, Montevideo

## USA

**Embassy** – Grosvenor Square, London W1A 1AE. Tel: (020) 7499 9000

**Consulate** – 5 Upper Grosvenor Street, London W1A 2JB. Tel: (020) 7499 3443

**British Embassy** – 3100 Massachusetts Avenue NW, Washington, DC 20008

**American Exchange Foundation** – 34 Belgrave Rd, Seaford, E. Sussex

**US–UK Educational Commission** – 62 Doughty Street, London WC1N 2LS. Tel: (020) 7404 6994

## Other school contacts

- Academia Language School, 1600 Kapiolani Blvd, Suite 1215, Honolulu, HI 96814
- Albert Magnus College, 811a Winchester Ave, Weldon, New Haven, CT 06511-1189
- American English Institute, California State U-Fresno, 2450 E San Ramon Ave, Room 138, Fresno, CA 93740-8032
- American Language Academy, Butler University, 750 West Hampton, Schwitzer Hall/B1, Indianapolis, IN 46208
- American Language Academy, University of Tampa, Box 39F, Tampa, FL 33606-1490
- American Language Institute, San Francsico State University, 1600 Holloway Ave, San Francsico, CA 94132. Tel: (415) 338-1438

## VENEZUELA

**Embassy** – 1 Cromwell Road, London SW7 2HW. Tel: (020) 7581 4206

**British Council** – Torre la Noria, Piso 6, Paseo Enrique Eraso, Las Mercedes/Sector San Román, Apartado 65131, Caracas 1065. Tel: (2) 915222
**Ministry of Education** – Edificio Educación, Esq El Conde, Caracas
**inLingua** – Avenida Urdaneta, Quinta No 13, Valencia
**Berlitz** – Av. Madrid, Urb. Las Mercedes, Caracas 1060

## Other school contacts

- Academia Jefferson, Calle T con D, Urb. Colinas de Valle Arriba, Caracas
- Childrens World, Quinta Santa Ana, Sorocaima, Urb. La Trinidad, Caracas
- Madison Learning Centre, Pre-school, Quinta Amaer, Calle Soledad, El Cafetal
- Madison Learning Centre, Primary-HS, Quinta Morelera, Calle Carupano and Calle El Morao, El Cafetal
- Christian Day Nursery, United Christian Church, Av. la Arboleda, Urb. El Bosque, Caracas
- Colegio Internacional de Carabobo, Apartado 103, Valencia

## VIETNAM

**Embassy** – 12 Victoria Road, London W8 5RD. Tel: (020) 7937 1912
**British Council** – 18b Cao Ba Quat, Ba Dinh District, Hanoi
25 Le Duan Street, District 1, Ho Chi Minh City (Saigon)
**Ministry of Education** – 21 Le Thanh Tong, Hanoi

## Other school contacts

- Apollo Education Centre, 191 Tay Son, Dong da, Hanoi. Email: Apollo@netnam.org.vn
- Centre for External Professionalism and Expertise, Cooperation and Exchange, 14 Le Thanh Tong, Hanoi
- Ho Chi Minh University of Education, Foreign Language Centre, 280 An Duong Vuong St, District 5, Ho Chi Minh City
- B.E.S.T. Services, (Better English Skills Today), 81A Nguyen Son Ha St, Ward 5, District 3, Ho Chi Minh City. Email: best-vn@hcm.vnn.vn
- Hanoi University for Foreign Study, Km 8, Nguyen Trai Rd, Hanoi
- International English School, 101C Nguyen Van Cu St, District 5, Ho Chi Minh City

## YEMEN

**Embassy** – 57 Cromwell Road, London SW7 2ED. Tel: (020) 7584 6607
**British Council** – House 7, Street 70, PO Box 2157, Sana'a. Tel: (1) 244121/2
Ho Chi Minh Street, PO Box 6170, Khormasksar, Aden
**Ministry of Education** – Sana'a

### Other school contacts

- Al Farouq Institute, PO Box 16927, Sana'a
- Faculty of Education, English Dept, PO Box 70270, Ibb
- Pakistani School, Sana'a
- University of Al-Ahgaff, PO Box 50341, Sana'a
- English Language Centre, PO Box 8984, Sana'a
- Madina Institute of Technology (MIT), Aden

## YUGOSLAVIA

**Embassy** – 5 Lexham Gardens, London W8 5JU. Tel: (020) 7370 6105
**British Council** – General Zdanova 34, 11001 Belgrade
**inLingua** – Ratka Pavlovica 13, (Vinogradi), 34000 Kragujevac

### Other school contacts

- ABC Centar, D.Obradovica 38, 21205 Sremski Karlovci. Email: radmil@eunet.yu
- Olympos, Bastinska 16, 2500 Sombor
- Lingva, Njegoseva 59, 11000 Beograd
- English Teaching Centre, Ljubicka 48, 32000 Cacak
- Forum, Jna 1, TC 'Trubac' II Sprat, 26000 Pancevo
- Anglia, Carli Caplina 37A, 11000 Beograd

# Acronyms and Terminology in TEFL and Education

The following list of terms commonly used in the world of TEFL, and General Education, should be of use to you when deciphering job advertisements and teaching documentation.

**ALL:** Association for Language Learning
**ALTE:** Association of Language Testers in Europe
**AE:** Adult Education
**ARELS:** Association of Recognised English Language Services
**ATT:** Association for Teacher Training (Ireland)
**BAAL:** British Association for Applied Linguistics
**BASELT:** British Association of State English Language Teaching
**BC:** British Council
**BECTA:** British Educational Communications and Technology Agency
**CAE:** Certificate in Advanced English (Cambridge)
**CBEVE:** Central Bureau for Educational Visits and Exchange
**CALL:** Computer Assisted Language Learning
**CELTA:** Certificate in English Language Teaching to Adults (Cambridge)
**CLA:** Copyright Licensing Agency
**CfBT:** Centre for British Teachers
**CPE:** Certificate of Proficiency in English (Cambridge)
**CILT:** Centre for Information on Language Teaching and Research
**DELTA:** Diploma in English Language Teaching to Adults (Cambridge)
**DfEE:** Department for Education and Employment
**DOS:** Director of Studies
**ELC:** European Language Council
**ECIS:** European Council of International Schools
**ESU:** English Speaking Union
**FCE:** First Certificate in English (Cambridge)
**FE:** Further Education

**FIPLV:** Fédération Internationale des Professeurs de Langues Vivantes
**GNVQ:** General National Vocational Qualification
**GCE:** General Certificate of Education (A-level)
**GCSE:** General Certificate of Secondary Education
**HE:** Higher Education
**IATEFL:** International Association of Teachers of EFL
**ICT:** Information and Communications Technology
**IB:** International Baccalaureate
**IELTS:** International English Language Testing Service
**IoL:** Institute of Linguists
**IGCSE:** International GCSE
**ITE:** Initial Teacher Education
**LEA:** Local Education Authority
**LNTO:** Languages National Training Organisation
**JALT:** Japan Association for Language Teaching
**JET:** Japanese Exchange and Teaching Programme
**KET:** Key English Test (Cambridge)
**L1:** First Language
**LCCIEB:** London Chamber of Commerce and Industry Examinations Board
**NALA:** National Association of Language Advisers
**NATE:** National Association for the Teaching of English
**NATECLA:** National Association for the Teaching of English and Community Languages to Adults
**NEC:** National Extension College
**NIACE:** National Institute of Adult Continuing Education
**NVQ:** National Vocational Qualification
**PET:** Preliminary English Test (Cambridge)
**ODA:** Overseas Development Agency
**OFSTED:** Office for Standards in Education
**OU:** Open University
**PGCE:** Postgraduate Certificate in Education
**QTS:** Qualified Teacher Status
**RELSA:** Recognised English Language Schools Association (Ireland)
**RSA:** Royal Society of Arts
**SALT:** Scottish Association for Language Teaching
**SCOTTESOL:** Scottish TESOL Assoc.
**TOEFL:** Test of English as a Foreign Language
**UETESOL:** University Entrance Test for Speakers of Other Languages

# Further Reading

## COUNTRIES AND REGIONS

Culture Shock! Guides to various countries (Kuperard)

How to Books series, living and working in various countries (How To Books)

*Live and Work in Central America*, Avril Harper (Grant Dawson 1991)

*Jobs in Japan*, J Wharton (Global Press/Vacation Work)

Live and Work in various countries, Vacation Work series

*Living and Working in Europe*, E Cobbe & J Maccarthaigh (Gill & Macmillan 1992)

Living and working in various countries, Survival Books series

Living in various countries, Robert Hale series

Long Stays series, David & Charles

*Setting up in Italy*, Sebastian O'Kelly (Merehurst 1990)

*Setting up in Spain*, David Hewson (Merehurst 1990)

*Working in the European Community*, A J Raban & William Archer (Hobsons 1995)

The *Daily Telegraph Guide to Working and Living Abroad*, Geoffrey Golzen (annual)

Volunteer work: the complete international guide to medium and long-term voluntary service, Central Bureau

## EDUCATION AND TEACHING

*A Course in Language Teaching*, Penny Ur (CUP 1996)

*Classroom Dynamics*, Jill Hadfield (OUP 1992)

*Education in Central America and the Caribbean*, C Brock & D Clarkson (Routledge 1990)

*Educational Innovation in China*, K Lewin et al. (Longman 1994)

*English in Asia*, John Wharton (Global Press)

*Essentials of English Language Teaching*, Julian Edge (Addison Wesley Longman 1993)

*Essential Teaching Skills*, Chris Kyriacou (Stanley Thornes 1998)
*Exam Classes*, Peter May (OUP 1996)
*A Handbook for Teaching English at Japanese Colleges and Universities*, Paul Wadden (OUP 1993)
*How Chinese Managers Learn*, Malcolm Warner (Macmillan 1992)
*Japan and Education*, Michael Stephens (Macmillan 1991)
*Producing Teaching Materials*, Phil Race & H Ellington (Kogan Page 1993)
*The Schooling of China*, John Cleverley (Allen & Unwin 1991)
*Teaching English Abroad*, Susan Griffith (Vacation Work 1997)
*Teaching English in Asia* (Vacation Work)
*Teaching English in Eastern and Central Europe*, Robert Lynes (In Print 1995)
*Teaching English in Italy*, Martin Penner (In Print 1994)
*Teaching English in South East Asia*, Nuala O'Sullivan (In Print 1997)
*Teaching English Overseas: An Introduction*, Sandra Lee McKay (OUP 1992)
*Theories of Educational Management*, Bush (Paul Chapman 1995)
*500 Tips for TESOL*, Sue Wharton & Phil Race (Kogan Page 1999)
*500 Computing Tips for Teachers and Learners*, Phil Race & Steve McDowell (Kogan Page 1996)

## GENERAL AND REFERENCE

*The Directory* (European Council for International Schools)
*The EARLS Guide to Language Schools in Europe* (EARLS)
*English in the National Curriculum*, Department for Education/ Welsh Office (HMSO 1995)
*English Language Teaching Guide* (*EL Gazette*, annual)
*Getting a Job Abroad*, Roger Jones (How To Books 1998)
*How to Master Languages*, Roger Jones (How to Books 1993)
*Living and Working Abroad – A Wife's Guide* (Kuperard 1997)
*Living and Working abroad – A Parent's Guide* (Kuperard 1997)
*Obtaining Visas and Work Permits*, Roger Jones (How To Books 1996)
*Speaking in Public: A Guide to Speaking with Confidence*, L Bostock (HarperCollins 1994)
*Travellers Handbook*, J Gorman ed. (WEXAS 1992)
*Travellers Health*, Richard Dawood (OUP)
*Travellers World Guides* to various countries (Trade & Travel

Publications)

*Working Abroad: Essential Financial Planning for Expatriates*, Jonathan Golding (International Venture Handbooks 1993)

*Working Holidays* (Central Bureau, annual)

*The World of Learning* (Europa, annual)

*The Internet Guide for English Language Teachers*, Sperling (Prentice Hall 1998)

*Accreditation in Basic Skills and ESOL: Information Pack*, ESOL syllabus design, produced by the London Language and Literacy Unit (see page 183)

*Adult ESOL Learners in Britain*, A L Khanna et al. (Multilingual Matters)

*Mainstreaming ESL*, John Clegg ed. (Multilingual Matters)

*English in Britain* (annual), produced by BASELT (see page 184)

*International Directory of Voluntary Work*, Vacation Work 1993

*Directory of Jobs and Careers Abroad*, Vacation Work 1993

## PERIODICALS AND JOURNALS

*Comparative Education Review* (Carfax Publishing Co., PO Box 25, Abingdon, Oxon OX14 3UE). Articles on educational development and book reviews.

*EL Gazette* – monthly on subscription (includes *El Prospects*) (details given in Chapter 1)

*ELT News and Views* (Uruguay 782–3, 1015 Capital, Buenos Aires, Argentina)

*English Language Teaching Journal* (OUP, Walton Street, Oxford OX2 6DP)

*English Today* (Cambridge University Press, The Edinburgh Building, Shaftesbury Road, Cambridge CB2 2RU)

*Home and Away* (on subscription from Expats International), 29 Lacon Road, London SE22 9HE.

*Jobfinder* (Overseas Consultants, PO Box 152, Isle of Man)

*Nexus* (Expat Network, International House, 500 Purley Way, Croydon, Surrey CR0 4NZ)

*Overseas Jobs Express* (Island Publishing, Premier House, Shoreham Airport BN43 5FF)

*Pay Away* (Ransom Publications, 57 Dafforne Road, Tooting Bec, London SW17 8TY)

*Resident Abroad* (Greystoke Place, Fetter Lane, London EC4A 1ND)

*The International Educator* (*TIE*), 102A Popes Lane, London W5
   4NS. Email: tie@capecod.net Web site: *www.tieonline.com*
*Times Educational Supplement*
*Times Higher Educational Supplement*
*TESOL Matters/TESOL Quarterly* (subscribers of TESOL associa-
   tion)

## TEFL RESOURCES

A selection of the most popular books in circulation and use (NB.
EFL coursebooks not included).

*The Practice of English Language Teaching*, Jeremy Harmer
   (Longman)
*Learning Teaching*, J Scrivener (Heinemann)
*Grammar Practice Activities*, Penny Ur (CUP)
*1000 pictures for Teachers to Copy*, Andrew Wright (Longman)
*Communication Games*, J Hadfield (Longman)
*A Practical Handbook of Language Teaching*, David Cross (Phoenix)
*Recipes for Tired Teachers*, Christopher Sion ed. (Addison Wesley
   Longman)
*How to Teach English*, Jeremy Harmer (Longman)
*An Introduction to English Language Teaching*, John Haycraft
   (Longman)
Cambridge University Press series of handbooks for Language
   Teachers, including *The Standby Book*, Seth Lindstromberg ed.
Teacher Development Series, from Macmillan Heinemann
*English Grammar in Use*, Raymond Murphy (CUP), now available
   with Supplentary Exercises book
*Practical English Usage*, Michael Swan (OUP)
*English Vocabulary in Use*, Stuart Redman (CUP)
*Practical English Grammar*, A J Thomson & N McLeod (OUP)
Vocabulary games series by Peter Watcyn-Jones (Penguin)
*The FCE Grammar Rom, and Grammar Rom Specimen Exams*,
   Ingrid Freebairn & Hilary Rees-Parnall (Longman 2000)

## USEFUL WEBSITES

BBC World Service                *http://bbc.co.uk/worldservice*
Central European Training
   Program                       *www.beloit.edu/~cetp*

| | |
|---|---|
| Digital Education Network | *http://www.edunet.com* |
| FIELS | *www.fiels.co.nz* |
| NZEIL | *www.nzeil.co.nz* |
| Project Trust | *Projecttrust.org.uk* |
| TESOL | *http://www.tesol.edu/* |
| VSO | *http://www.oneworld.org/vso/* |
| Language Learning Resource | |
|   Centre | *http://ml.hss.cmu.edu/llrc* |
| Dave's ESL café | *http://www.pacificnet.net/~sperling/* |
| | *eslcafe.html* |
| ESL resources | *http://deil.lang.uiuc.edu/LinguaCenter* |
| Webster's dictionary | *http://humanities.uchicago.edu/forms* |
| | *_unrest/webster.form.html* |
| Rhyming dictionary | *http://bobo.link.cs.cmu.edu/cgi-bin/* |
| | *dougb/rhyme.cgi* |
| Britspeak (US/UK English) | *http://pages.prodigy.com/NY/NYC/* |
| | *britspk/main.html* |
| English usage/style | *http://www.theslot.com/contents.html* |
| Focus on words | *http://www.wordfocus.com/* |
| Intro to TEFL | *http://www.edunet.com/nec/* |
| Word play | *http://homepage.interaccess.com/* |
| | *~wolinsky/word.htm* |
| World Wide Words | *http://clever.net/quinion/words/* |
| | *index.htm* |
| EFL mag online | *http://www.u-net.com/eflweb/* |
| The Telegraph | *http://www.telegraph.co.uk* |
| Welcome to Britain | *http://openworld.co.uk/britain* |
| Excite City Net | *http://www.city.net* |
| The Open University | *http://www.open.ac.uk* |
| Childrens Literature page | *http://www.ucalgary.ca/~dkbrown/* |
| | *index.html* |
| IATEFL | *http://www.iatefl.org* |
| Longman EFL publications | *http://www.longman-elt.com* |

# Useful Contacts

These contacts are in addition to any already mentioned in the main part of the book. The list is not exhaustive and further information can always be sought from the relevant departments and bodies.

## OFFICIALDOM

**Blair Consular Services** (Visas), 9 City Business Centre, Lower Rd, London SE16 2XB. Tel: (020) 7252 1451.

**Commonwealth Information Centre**, Commonwealth Institute, Kensington High St, London W8 6NQ. Tel: (020) 7603 4535

**European Commission Office**, 8 Storey Gate, London SW1P 3AT. Tel: (020) 7973 1992. Fax: (020) 7973 1900

**FCO Travel Advice Unit**, Consular Dept, Clive House, Petty France, London SW1H 9HD. Tel: (020) 7270 4129

**Ministry of Agriculture**, Animal Health Division IC (taking pets abroad), Hook Rise South, Tolworth, Surbiton, Surrey KT6 7NF. Tel: (020) 8330 4441

**Ministry of Agriculture, Fisheries and Food**, Nobel House, 17 Smith Square, London SW1P 3HX. Tel: (020) 7238 3000

## VOLUNTARY AND OTHER AGENCIES

**Action Partners**, Bawtry Hall, South Parade, Bawtry, Doncaster DN10 6JH. Tel: (01302) 710750. Fax: (01302) 719399. Email: actionpartners.@org.uk

**Africa Evangelical Fellowship**, 6 Station Court, Station Approach, Borough Green, Sevenoaks TN15 8AD. Tel: (01732) 885590. Fax: (01732) 882990. Email: 100635.2043@compuserve.com Web site: *www.netaccess.on.ca/~sma/gallery/aef/display/display.htm*

**Africa Inland Mission**, 2 Vorley Rd, London N19 5HE. Tel: (020) 8281 1184. Email: africa.mission@ukonline.co.uk

**Agency for Personal Service Overseas**, 29–30 Fitzwilliam Square, Dublin 2, Ireland. Tel: (1) 661 4411. Fax: (1) 661 4202. Email: apso@iol.ie.

**Baptist Missionary Society**, PO Box 49, 129 Broadway, Didcot OX11 8XA. Tel: (01235) 512077. Fax: (01235) 511265

**Christians Abroad**, 1 Stockwell Green, London SW9 9HP. Tel: (020) 7737 7811. Fax: (020) 7737 3237

**Church of Scotland** (World Mission and Unity), 121 George St, Edinburgh EH2 4YN. Tel: (0131) 225 5722. Fax: (0131) 226 6121. Email: kirkworldlink@gn.apc.org.

**Crosslinks**, 251 Lewisham Way, London SE4 1XF. Tel: (020) 8691 6111

**Department for International Development**, Abercrombie House, Eaglesham Rd, East Kilbride G75 8EA. Tel: (01355) 844000. Email: recruitment-enqs@dfid.gtnet.gov.uk.
Web site: *www.oneworld.org/dfid*

**i to i International Projects Ltd**, 1 Cottage Rd, Headingley, Leeds LS6 4DD. Tel: (0113) 217 9800. Fax: (0113) 217 9801.
Email: info@i-to-i.com. Website: *www.i-to-i.com/iventure*

**Interserve**, 325 Kennington Rd, London SE11 4QH. Tel: (020) 7735 8227. Fax: (020) 7587 5362.
Email: 100014.2566@compuserve.com

**JET Programme** (Japan Exchange and Teaching), The Council for International Exchange, 33 Seymour Place, London W1H 6AT. Tel: (020) 7224 8896

**Methodist Church**, World Church Office, 25 Marylebone Rd, London NW1 5JR. Tel: (020) 7486 5502. Fax: (020) 7935 1507

**Refugee Council**, Bondway House, 3–9 Bondway, London SW8 1SJ. Tel: (020) 7820 3000

**SIM UK**, Ullswater Crescent, Colsdon, Surrey CR5 2HR. Tel/fax: (020) 8660 7778. Email: postmaster@sim.co.uk.
Web site: *www.sim.org*.

**Skillshare Africa**, 126 New Walk, Leicester LE1 7JA. Tel: (0116) 254 1862. Fax: (0116) 254 2614.
Email: skillshare-uk@geo2.poptel.org.uk.

**South American Missionary Society**, Unit 1, Prospect Business Park, Langston Rd, Loughton IG10 3TZ. Tel/fax: (020) 8502 3504. Email: 101607.507@compuserve.com

**Teaching Abroad Ltd**, Gerrard House, Rustington, West Sussex BN16 1AW. Tel: (01903) 859911. Fax: (01903) 785779.
Email: teaching_abroad@garlands.uk.com
Web site: *www.teaching-abroad.co.uk*.

**The East European Partnership**, (VSO) Carlton House, 27A Carlton Drive, London SW15 2BS. Tel: (020) 8780 2841. Fax: (020) 8780 9592

**Volunteer Missionary Movement**, 1 Stockwell Green, London SW9 9JF. Tel: (020) 7737 3678. Fax: (020) 7737 3237. Email: vmmevago@iol.ie

**VSO**, 317 Putney Bridge Rd, London SW15 2PN. Tel: (020) 8780 2266. Fax: (020) 8780 1326

**World Church and Mission**, United Reformed Church, 86 Tavistock Place, London WC1H 9RD. Tel: (020) 7916 2020. Fax: (020) 7916 2021

## RECRUITMENT SERVICES

**CEPEC Ltd**, 67 Jermyn St, London SW1Y 6NY. Tel: (020) 7930 0322

**Crown Agents**, International Recruitment Division, St Nicholas House, St Nicholas Rd, Sutton SM1 1EL. Tel: (020) 8643 3311. Fax: (020) 8643 9331. Email: crownagents@attmail.com

**Eagle Recruitment**, 57 Brompton Rd, London SW3 1DP. Tel: (020) 7823 9233

**ELT Banbury**, 49 Oxford Rd, Banbury, Oxfordshire OX16 9AH. Tel: (01295) 263502. Fax: (01295) 271658

**English World-Wide**, The Italian Building, Dockhead, London SE1 2BS. Tel: (020) 7252 1402. Fax: (020) 7231 8002

**FRES Federation of Recruitment and Employment Services Ltd**, 36–38 Mortimer St, London W1N 7RB

**Gabbitas Educational Consultants**, Carrington House, 126–130 Regent St, London W1R 6EE. Tel: (020) 7439 2071. Fax: (020) 7437 1764

**ILC Recruitment**, White Rock, Hastings, East Sussex TN43 1JY. Tel: (01424) 720109. Fax: (01424) 720323

**Network Overseas**, 34 Mortimer St, London W1N 8JR. Tel: (020) 7580 5151. Fax: (020) 7580 6242. Email: network@network.sonnet.co.uk Web site: *www.sonnet.co.uk/network*

**Nord Anglia International**, 10 Eden Place, Cheadle, Stockport, Cheshire SK8 1AT. Tel: (0161) 491 4191. Email: 100532.40@compuserve.com

**PACES Recruitment Services**, PO Box 232, Redhill, Surrey RH1 8YP. Tel/Fax: (01833) 744558.

**Publicitas Ltd**, 525 Fulham Rd, London SW6. Tel: (020) 7385 7723

**Recruitment International**, International House, PO Box 300, Harrogate, North Yorks HG1 5XL. Tel: (01423) 530533. Fax: (01423) 530558. Email: ri_group@compuserve.com

**Saxoncourt Recruitment**, Norman House, 105–109 The Strand, London WC2R 0AA. Tel: (020) 7836 1567. Fax: (020) 7836 1789 Email: recruit@saxoncourt.com Web site: *www.saxoncourt.com*

**Skola Recruitment**, 21 Star St, London W2 1QB. Tel: (020) 7387 0656. Fax: (020) 7724 2219

**Specialist Language Services**, 7 Marsden Business Park, Clifton, York YO3 4XG. Tel: (01904) 691313. Fax: (01904) 691102. Email: admin@slsyork.co.uk

**Timeplan Education Group Ltd**, 20/21 Arcadia Ave, London N3 2JU. Tel: (020) 371 8030/ and 307 West George St, Glasgow G2 4LF. Tel: (0141) 204 5800. Fax: (0141) 204 5900.
Web site: *www.timeplan.com*

**Worldwide Educational Service**, Canada House, 272 Field End Rd, Eastcote, Ruislip HA4 9NA. Tel: (020) 8582 0317. Fax: (020) 8582 0320. Email: wes@wesworldwide.com
Web site: *www.wesworldwide.com*

## TRAVEL

**British Rail Continental Section**, Victoria Station, London SW1. Tel: (020) 7834 2345

**British Airways Travel Clinic**, 156 Regent St, London W1R 5TA. Tel: (020) 7831 5333 (plus other locations)

**British Tourist Authority/English Tourist Board**, Thames Tower, Blacks Rd, London W6 9EL. Tel: (020) 8846 9000. Fax: (020) 8563 0302. Web site: *www.bta.org.uk*

**Brittany Ferries**, Millbay Docks, Plymouth, Devon PL1 3EW. Tel: 0990 360360

**P&O European Ferries**, The Continental Ferry Port, Mile End, Portsmouth PO2 8QW. Tel: 0990 980980

**Spratts Animal Travel Service**, 756 High Rd, Goodmayes, Ilford, Essex IG3 8SY. Tel: (020) 8597 2415

## REMOVALS

**Avalon Overseas**, Drury Way, Brent Park, London NW10 0JN. Tel: (020) 8451 6336. Fax: (020) 8451 6419.
Email: avalon@transeuro.com

**Bishops Move**, Overseas House, Stewarts Rd, London SW8 4UG. Tel: (020) 7498 0300. Fax: (020) 7498 0749. Email: www.bishopsmove.co.uk

**Britannia**, Unit 3, Wyvern Estate, Beverley Way, New Maldern, Surrey KT3 4PH. Tel: (020) 8336 0220. Fax: (020) 8336 0961. Email: www.britannia_movers.co.uk

**Charles M Willie & Co. (Shipping) Ltd**, Celtic House, Brittania Rd, Cardiff CF1 5LS. Tel: (029) 20471000

**Copsey Removals**, 178 Crow Lane, Romford, Essex RM7 0ES. Tel: (020) 8592 1003. Fax: (01708) 727305

**Ferry Freighting (Manchester) Ltd**, Ferry House, 24–26 Brook St, Chedderton, Oldham OL9 6NN. Tel: (0161) 626 8686

**Fleet Shipping International Ltd**, Tel: (020) 7232 0777. Fax: (020) 7232 2600. Email: sales@fleet.demon.co.uk Web site: *www.fleet-shipping.co.uk*

**Gauntlett International Removals Ltd**, Gauntlett House, Catteshall Rd, Godalming, Surrey GU7 1NH. Tel: (01483) 417766

**Northovers Removals and Storage**, Passfield Mill Business Park, Passfield, near Liphook, Hants GU30 7RR. Tel: (01428) 751554. Fax: (01428) 751564

**Overs International**, Unit 8, Government Road Industrial Park, Government Rd, Aldershot GU11 2DA. Tel: (01252) 343646. Fax: (01252) 345861

**Robert Darvall Ltd**, 4 Acre Road, Reading, Berkshire RG1 0SX. Tel: (01734) 864422

**The British Association of Removers**, 3 Churchill Court, 58 Station Road, North Harrow, Middlesex HA2 7SA. Tel: (020) 8861 3331. Fax: (020) 8861 3332. Email: movers@bar.co.uk

**The Old House (Removals and Warehousing) Ltd**, London. Tel: (020) 8947 1817. Also at: 15–17 High Street, Seaford, East Sussex BN25 1PD. Tel: (01323) 892934

## ACCOMMODATION

**Homesitters Ltd**, The Old Bakery, Western Rd, Tring, Herts HP23 4BB. Tel: (01442) 891188

**Youth Hostels Association**, 14 Southampton St, London WC2.

## PROPERTY AGENTS

**Aimcliff Properties**, 5–9 Station Rd, Hornchurch, Essex RM12 6JL. Tel: (020) 7435 1480. Fax: (020) 7435 1478

**Cambridge Trading International Ltd**, 83–85 Dunstable Street, Ampthill, Bedford MK45 2NQ. Tel: (01525) 405900

**Jones Lang Wootton**, 22 Hanover Square, London W1A 2BN. Tel: (020) 7493 6040. Fax: (020) 7493 9539

**Mike Hough Associates (Agricultural)**, The Laurels, Mill Road, Bintree, Dereham, Norfolk NR20 5NL. Tel: (01362) 683790. Fax: (01362) 684175

**Prime Property International**, 7 High St, Maidenhead, Berkshire SL6 1JN. Tel: (01628) 778841. Fax: (01628) 35052

**Pugh Homes**, 42 Walcott Av, Christchurch, Dorset BH23 2NG. Tel/Fax: (01202) 487396

**Roy Grant & Co.**, 1 Albert St, Aberdeen AB1 1XX. Tel: (01224) 645066. Fax: (01224) 642525

## FINANCIAL

**Allan Wright (Canada Life Assurance Co)**, Albany House, Dollis Mews, Dollis Park, Finchley, London N3 1HH. Tel: (020) 8346 2651

**Blackstone Franks**, Barbican House, 26–34 Old Street, London EC1V 9HL. Tel: (020) 7250 3300

**Bone & Co. Insurance Brokers**, 69A Castle St, Farnham, Surrey GU9 7LP. Tel: (01252) 724140

**Brown Shipley Lomond Ltd**, 84 Coombe Rd, New Malden, Surrey KT3 4QS. Tel: (020) 8949 8811

**Dave Tester Expatriate Insurance Services**, 18A Hove Park Villas, Hove BN3 6HG. Tel: (01273) 703469. Fax: (01273) 777723. Email: dave.tester@compuserve.com

**Expat Tax Consultants**, Churchfield House, North Drive, Hebburn, Tyne & Wear NE31 1ES. Tel: (0191) 483 7805

**Expatriate Advisory Services**, 14 Gordon Rd, West Bridgeford, Nottingham NG2 5LN. Tel: (01602) 816572

**Expats International**, 29 Lacon Rd, London SE22 9HE. Tel: (020) 8229 2484

**Hall-Godwins Overseas**, Briarcliff House, Kingsmead, Farnborough, Hants GU14 7TE. Tel: (01252) 521701

**Ronald M Collins & Co**, Chartered Accountants, Downs Court Business Centre, 29 The Downs, Altrincham, Cheshire WA14 2QD. Tel: (0161) 941 2868

**Seatax Ltd** (tax advisers), 100 East Iaith Gate, Doncaster DN1 1JA. Tel: (01302) 364673

**Wilfred T. Fry Ltd**, Crescent House, Crescent Rd, Worthing BN11 1RN. Tel: (01903) 231545. Fax: (01903) 200868

## BANKS

**Barclays Bank Plc**, International Banking Group, 168 Fenchurch Street, London EC3P 3HP. Tel: (020) 7283 8989
**The Bank of England**, Threadneedle St, London EC2R 8AH. Tel: (020) 7601 4444

## TAX/WORK DEPARTMENTS

**Department for Education and Employment** (DfEE), Sanctuary Buildings, Great Smith Street, London SW1P 3BT. Tel: (020) 7925 5555. Email: info@dfee.gov.uk
**Employment Services**, Overseas Placing Unit, (OPS5), Moorfoot, Sheffield, S1 4PQ.
**Inland Revenue Claims Branch**, Foreign Division, Merton Rd, Bootle L69 9BL. Tel: (0151) 922 6363
**Inland Revenue**, Inspector of Foreign Dividends, Lynwood Rd, Thames Ditton, Surrey.

## HEALTH

**BUPA International**, Russell Mews, Brighton BN7 2NE. Tel: (01273) 208181. Fax: (01273) 866583. Web site: *www.bupa.com/int*
**Department of Health Leaflets Unit**, PO Box 21, Honeypot Lane, Stanmore, Middlesex HA7 1AY. Tel: 0800 555777
**DSS Benefits Agency**, Pensions & Overseas Benefits Directorate, Incapacity Benefits Section, Tyneview Park, Whitely Rd, Newcastle-upon-Tyne NE98 1BA
**Exeter Friendly Society** (Medical Insurance), Beech Hill, Walnut Gardens, Exeter, Devon EX4 4DG. Tel: (01392) 477210
**Harley Medical Services**, 177A Harley St, London W1N 1DH. Tel: (020) 7935 1536
**Healthsearch Ltd** (medical insurance advice), 9 Newland St, Rugby CV22 7BJ. Tel: (01788) 541855
**Medical Advisory Services for Travellers Abroad Ltd** (MASTA), Bureau of Hygiene & Tropical Medicine, Keppel St, London WC1E 7HT. Tel: (020) 7631 4408

**PPP**, Eynsham House, Tunbridge Wells, Kent TN1 2PL. Tel: (01892) 512345

**RNIB**, Head Office, 224 Great Portland St, London W1N 6AA. Tel: (020) 7388 1266. Fax: (020) 7388 2034

**Royal National Institute for Deaf People**, 19–23 Featherstone St, London EC1Y 8SL. Tel: (020) 7296 8000. Fax: (020) 7296 8199. Minicom: (020) 7296 8001

**Social Security Agency**, Incapacity Benefits Branch, Castle Court, Royal Ave, Belfast BT1 1UB

## ACCOUNTANCY FIRMS

**Arthur Andersen & Co.**, 1 Surrey St, London WC2R 2PS. Tel: (020) 7438 3000

**Ernst & Young**, Rolls House, 7 Rolls Buildings, Fetter Lane, London EC4A 1NH. Tel: (020) 7831 7130

**KPMG Peat Marwick**, 1 Puddle Dock, Blackfriars, London EC4V 3PD. Tel: (020) 7236 8000

## DRIVING

**AA**, Fanum House, Basingstoke, Hampshire RG21 2EA

**Manor Car Storage**, PO Box 28, Clavering, Saffron Walden, Essex CB11 4RA. Tel: (01799) 550021

**RAC**, Landsdowne Rd, Croydon, Surrey CR9 2JA

## EDUCATION

**ALAOME** (Association of LEA Advisory Officers for Multicultural Education), c/o MECSS, Education Dept, County Hall, Hertford SG13 8DF. Tel: (01992) 555926/7. Fax: (01992) 555925

**Basic Skills Agency, Commonwealth House**, 1–19 New Oxford St, London WC1A 1NU. Tel: (020) 7405 4017. Fax: (020) 7405 5038

**BBC Broadcasting Support Services**, 252 Western Ave, London W3 6WJ. Tel: (020) 7992 5522

**European Council of International Schools**, 21b Lavant Street, Petersfield, Hants. GU2 3EL. Tel: (01730) 268244. Email: ecis@ecis.org

**London Language and Literacy Unit**, Southwark College, Southampton Way, London SE5 7EW. Tel: (020) 7639 9512

**Open University**, PO Box 71, Walton Hall, Milton Keynes MK7 6AG. Tel: (01908) 74066

**Teacher Training Agency** (TTA), Portland House, Stag Place, London SW1E 5TT. Tel: (020) 7925 5880/5882

## LANGUAGE INFORMATION

**ABLS** (Association of British Language Schools), 8–10 Tudor Mews, 1 Hawthorn Rd, London NW10 2NE. Tel/Fax: (020) 7377 1737. Email: info@abls.co.uk

**ARELS** (Association of Recognised English Language Services), 2 Pontypool Place, Valentines Place, London SE1 8QF. Tel: (020) 7242 3136. Fax: (020) 7928 9378

**Association of Language Excellence Centres**, Garden Studios, 11–15 Betterton St, Covent Garden, London WC2H 9BP. Tel: (070) 4401 2532. Email: members@lxcentres.com

**Association of Translation Companies**, Alexandra House, Alexandra Terrace, Guildford GU1 3DA. Tel: (01483) 456486

**Association for Language Learning**, 150 Railway Terrace, Rugby CV21 3HN. Tel: (01788) 546443. Fax: (01788) 544149. Email: langlearn@aol.com

**BASELT** (British Association of State English Language Teaching), Cheltenham & Gloucester College of Higher Education, Francis Close Hall, Swindon Rd, Cheltenham GL50 4AZ. Tel: (01242) 227099. Fax: (01242) 227055

**BATQI** (British Association of TESOL Qualifying Institutions), 35 Barclay Square, Bristol BS8 1JA. Email: a.gilpin@bristol.ac.uk

**CfBT** (Centre for British Teachers), 1 The Chambers, East St, Reading RG1 4JD. Tel: (0118) 952 3900. Fax: (0118) 952 3939

**CILT** – Centre for Information on Language Teaching and Research, 20 Bedfordbury, London WC2N 4LB. Tel: (020) 7379 5110. Fax: (020) 7379 5082. Email: library@cilt.org.uk Web site: *www.cilt.org.uk*

**International Association of Teachers of EFL** (IATEFL), 3 Kingsdown Chambers, Kingsdown Park, Whitstable CT5 2DJ. Tel: (01227) 276528. Fax: (01227) 274415. Email: 100070.1327@compuserve.com Web site: *www.go-ed.com/jobs/iatefl*

**NATE** (National Association for the Teaching of English), 50 Broadfield Rd, Broadfield Business Centre, Sheffield S8 0XJ.

**NATECLA** (National Association for Teaching English and Community Languages to Adults), National Centre, South Birmingham College, 525 Stratford Rd, Birmingham B11 4AJ. Tel: (0121) 694 5000. Fax: (0121) 694 5007

**Scottish Association for Language Learning**, George Herriott School, Lauriston Place, Edinburgh EH3 9EQ. Tel: (0131) 229 7263

**SOAS** (School of Oriental and African Studies), Thornhaugh St, Russell Square, London WC1H 0XG. Tel: (020) 7637 2388

**The British Council Information Centre** (EFL), 5th Floor, Bridgewater House, 58 Whitworth St, Manchester M1 6BB. Tel: (0161) 957 7755. Fax: (0161) 957 7762.
Email: general.enquiries@britcoun.org
Web site: *www.britcoun.org*


## MAIN TEFL CHAIN GROUPS

**Bell Educational Trust**, Hillscross, Red Cross Lane, Cambridge CB2 2QX. Tel: (01223) 246644. Fax: (01223) 410282.
Email: lizc@bell-schools.ac.uk Web site: *www.bell-schools.ac.uk*

**Callan School of English**, Berwick House, 139 Oxford St, London W1R 1TD. Tel: (020) 7437 4573. Fax: (020) 7494 3204.
Email: 100345.3077@compuserve.com

**CfBT Education Services**, 1 The Chambers, East St, Reading RG1 4JD. Tel: (0118) 952 3900. Fax: (0118) 952 3924.
Email: intrecruit@cfbt-hq.org.uk Web site: *www.cfbt.com*

**ELT International**, 49 Oxford Rd, Banbury, Oxon OX16 9AH. Tel: (01295) 263480/263502. Fax: (01295) 271658.
Email: 100760.2247@compuserve.com

**English First Recruitment**, Box 5761, 114 87 Stockholm, Sweden. Tel: (95) 937 3887. Fax: (95) 937 3889. Email: elteacher@ef.com
Web site: *www.ef.com / www.englishtown.com*

**Inlingua Teacher Training and Recruitment**, Rodney Lodge, Rodney Rd, Cheltenham GL50 1JF. Tel: (01242) 253171. Fax: (01242) 253181. Email: training@inlingua-cheltenham.co.uk
Web site: *www.inlingua-cheltenham.co.uk*

**International House**, Staffing Unit, 106 Picadilly, London W1V 9FL. Tel: (020) 7491 2410. Fax: (020) 7491 2679.
Email: 100645.1547@compuserve.com
Web site: *www.international-house.org*

**Linguarama**, Oceanic House, 89 High St, Alton, Hants GU34 1LG. Tel: (01420) 80899. Fax: (01420) 80856.
Email: linguarama_alt@compuserve.com
Web site: *www.linguarama.com*

## GRANT BODIES

**Central Bureau**, 10 Spring Gardens, London SW1A 2BN. Tel: (020) 7389 4004. Fax: (020) 7389 4426

**DfEE**, Sanctuary Buildings, Great Smith St, London SW1P 3BT. Tel: (020) 7925 5555. (Bilingual GEST grants to train teachers of bilingual learners)

## EXAM BOARDS

**AQA**, incorporating NEAB/AEB/City & Guilds, Stag Hill House, Guildford, Surrey GU2 5XJ. Tel: (01483) 477 851. Fax: (01483) 455 736

**CENTRA**, Examinations and Assessments Services, Duxbury Park, Duxbury Hall Road, Chorley, Lancashire PR7 4AT. Tel: (01257) 241428. Fax: (01257) 260357

**Edexcel** (London Exam Board), incorporating BTec, Stewart House, 32 Russell Square, London WC1B 5DN. Tel: (020) 7331 4021. Fax: (020) 7331 4022

**English Speaking Board (International) Ltd**, 26a Princes St, Southport, Merseyside PR8 1EQ. Tel: (01704) 501730. Fax: (01704) 539637. Email: admin@esbuk.demon.co.uk
Web site: *www.esbuk.demon.co.uk*

**Institute of Linguists** (IoL), Saxon House, 48 Southwark St, London SE1 1UN. Tel: (020) 7940 3100. Fax: (020) 7940 3101

**LCCIEB** (London Chamber of Commerce and Industry Exam Board), 112 Station Rd, Sidcup, Kent DA15 7BJ. Tel: (020) 8302 0261. Fax: (020) 8302 4169. Email: custserv@lccieb.org.uk
Web site: *www.lccieb.org.uk*

**Trinity College London**, 16 Park Crescent, London W1N 4AP. Tel: (020) 7323 2328. Fax: (020) 7323 5201.
Email: info@trinitycollege.co.uk
Web site: *www.trinitycollege.co.uk*

**UCLES/RSA** (Cambridge Exams/Oxford Delegacy Exams), 1 Hills Rd, Cambridge CB1 2EU. Tel: (01223) 553311. Fax: (01223) 460278. Email: efl@ucles.org.uk Web site: *www.ucles.org.uk*

## CULTURAL

**BBC World Service**, PO Box 76, Bush House, Strand, London WC2B 4PH. Tel: (020) 7240 3456

**British Council (UK)**, 10 Spring Gardens, London SW1. Tel: (020) 7930 8466

**Centre for International Briefing**, Farnham Castle, Surrey GU9 0AG. Tel: (01252) 720416. Email: cibfarnham@dial.pipex.com Web site: *www.cibfarnham.com*

**Council of Europe**, Council for Cultural Co-operation (CDCC), Modern Languages Section, F-67075 Strasbourg Cedex, France. Tel: 33-3-88-41-2625. Email: philia.thalgott@decs.coe.fr

**Experiment in International Living**, Otesaga, West Malvern Rd, Malvern WR14 4EN. Tel: (016845) 62577

**Hosting for Overseas Students** (HOST), 18 Northumberland Ave, London WC2N 5BJ. Tel: (020) 7925 2595

## READING MATTER

**Consyl Publishing**, 3 Buckhurst Rd, Town Hall Square, Bexhill-on-Sea, Sussex TN40 1QF. Tel: (01424) 223111. Publish *Australian and New Zealand Outlook*

**EL Gazette**, Dilke House, 1 Malet St, London W1 7JA. Tel: (020) 7255 1969. Fax: (020) 7255 1972

**Outbound Newspapers Ltd**, 1 Commercial Rd, Eastbourne BN21 3XQ. Tel: (01323) 412001. Publishers of various newsletters about Australia, New Zealand, Canada, South Africa, USA.

**Suzy Lamplugh Trust** (info on safe travel abroad), 14 East Sheen Ave, London SW14 8AS. Tel: (020) 8392 1939.
Email: resources@suzylamplugh.org
Web site: *www.suzylamplugh.org/worldwise*

## BOOKSHOPS/LIBRARIES

**Bailey Bros & Swinfen Ltd**, Warner House, Folkestone, Kent CT19 6PH. Tel: (01303) 56501

**European Schoolbooks Ltd**, The Runnings, Cheltenham GL51 9PQ. Tel: (01242) 245252. Fax: (01242) 224137. Email: direct@esb.co.uk

**Good Book Guide**, 24 Seward St, London EC1V 3PS. Tel: (020) 7490 0900

**Grant & Cutler**, 55–57 Great Marlborough Street, London W1V 2AY. Tel: (020) 7734 2012. Fax: (020) 7734 9272.
Email: postmaster@grant-c.demon.co.uk

**Stanfords** (maps/travel), 12–14 Long Acre, Covent Garden, London WC2E 9LP. Tel: (020) 7836 1321. Fax: (020) 7836 0189.
Email: SALES@Stanfords.co.uk

**W & G Foyle**, 113–119 Charing Cross Rd, London WC2H 0EB. Tel: (020) 7437 5660

**British Library Newspaper Library**, Colindale Ave, London NW9 5HE. Tel: (020) 7412 7353. Fax: (020) 7412 7379.
Email: newspaper@bl.uk
Web site: *http://portico.bl.uk/newspaper*


## PUBLISHERS

**Addison Wesley Longman**, Edinburgh Gate, Harlow, Essex CM20 2JE. Tel: (01279) 623623. Fax: (01279) 623947.
Email: elt@awl.co.uk Web site: *www.awl-elt.com*

**Authentically English**, 85 Gloucester Road, London SW7 4SS. Tel: (020) 7244 7301. Fax: (020) 7835 0761.
Email: authentically.english@btinternet.com

**BBC English**, Room A3148, Woodlands, 80 Wood Lane, London W12 0TT. Tel: (020) 8576 3560. Fax: (020) 8576 3570

**Cambridge University Press** (CUP), The Edinburgh Building, Shaftesbury Rd, Cambridge CB2 2RU. Tel: (01223) 312393. Fax: (01223) 315052. Email: eltmail@cup.cam.ac.uk
Website: *www.cup.cam.ac.uk/elt*

**Camsoft** (CALL), 10 Wheatfield Close, Maidenhead, Berkshire SL6 3PS. Tel: (01628) 825206. Fax: (01628) 825206

**Collins Cobuild/HarperCollins**, 77–85 Fulham Palace Rd, Hammersmith, London W6 8JB. Tel: (020) 8307 4184. Fax: (020) 8307 4793. Email: info@cobuild.collins.co.uk
Web site: *www.cobuild.collins.co.uk*

**Connect ELT**, Unit B4, Dovers Farm, Reigate RH2 7XT. Tel: (01737) 225707. Fax: (01737) 225775. Email: nn39@dial.pipex.com
Web site: *www.connectelt.com*

**Dorling Kindersley Ltd**, 9 Henrietta Street, London WC2E 8PS. Tel: (020) 7836 5411. Fax: (020) 7836 7570

**Euro Talk Ltd** (CALL), 315-317 New Kings Road, Fulham, London SW6 4RF. Tel: (020) 7371 7711. Fax: (020) 7371 7781

**Harrap**, 45 Annandale Street, Edinburgh EH7 4AZ. Tel: (0131) 557 4571. Fax: (0131) 557 2936

**Heinemann ELT**, Halley Court, Jordan Hill, Oxford OX2 8EJ. Tel: (01865) 314292. Fax: (01865) 314193

**Hugos Language Books Ltd**, Old Station Yard, Marlesford, Woodbridge, Suffolk IP13 0AG. Tel: (01728) 746546. Fax: (01728) 746236

**Letts Educational**, Aldine Place, London W12 8AW. Tel: (020) 8740 2266. Fax: (020) 8743 8451. Email: mail@lettsed.co.uk Web site: *www.lettsed.co.uk*

**Macmillan Education Ltd**, Houndmills, Basingstoke, Hants. RG21 2XS. Tel: (01256) 29242. Fax: (01256) 814642

**Multilingual Matters**, Frankfurt Lodge, Clevedon Hall, Victoria Rd, Clevedon, North Somerset BS21 7SJ. Tel: (01275) 876519. Fax: (01275) 343096. Email: multi@multi.co.uk

**Oxford University Press** (OUP), Walton Street, Oxford OX2 6DP. Tel: (01865) 56767. Fax: (01865) 56646. Email: elt.enquiry@oup.co.uk Web site: *www.oup.co.uk/elt*

**Penguin Books Ltd**, 27 Wrights Lane, London W8 5TZ. Tel: (020) 7416 3000. Fax: (020) 7416 3099. Web site: *www.pcp.co.uk*

# Index